THE TIME HAS COME

Peter Sills

The Time Has Come

A LENTEN JOURNEY WITH ST MARK

the columbz press

First published in 2006 by
the columba press
55A Spruce Avenue, Stillorgan Industrial Park,
Blackrock, Co Dublin

Cover by Lisa Gifford
Origination by The Columba Press
Printed in Ireland by ColourBooks Ltd, Dublin

ISBN 1 85607 528 1

Acknowledgements
Biblical quotations are taken from *The Oxford Study Bible: Revised English Bible with Apocrypha,* copyright © 1992, Oxford University Press, New York. Used by permission. The quotation from *The Gospel according to St Mark* by C. F. D. Moule is used by permission of Cambridge University Press.

Table of Contents

For Helen

Preface

St Mark's gospel is one of the founding documents of the New Testament, and because of that it has held a particular fascination for me. There is an immediacy and a freshness about the language, and a humour – that remained hidden until I heard Alec McGowan's celebrated recitation of it. There are also profound insights into the character and message of Jesus that do not come through in quite the same way in the other gospels. Nor does Mark mince his words about the personal challenge of being a Christian. The radical obedience to God that Jesus expected is made plain, as is the power of God to take frail human nature and work through it.

This Lenten Journey with St Mark takes his gospel as it is and tries to let Mark's picture of Jesus stand out untrammelled by the pictures in the other gospels. It is not an easy read, and Jesus is not an easy person; but we do not live in easy times. Mark speaks to us today precisely because of this; as John Fenton has said, it is the best gospel for the twenty-first century because of the radical challenge that it poses to our modern ways and values. (John Fenton, *More about Mark*, p 58) So, as the journey unfolds I have drawn some parallels between the story Mark relates and our situation today, a situation compounded of political, economic and moral elements that point to our spiritual impoverishment which the time has come to redress.

I am very grateful to Bishop John Taylor, Dr Bridget Nicholls, and my wife Dr Helen Sills, for reading the text and offering many helpful comments. I should also like to thank Seán O Boyle of The Columba Press for his encouragement and support. I have acknowledged as many of the sources that have influenced me as I am aware, and, as will be apparent, I have gained much from the work of C. H. Dodd, Denis Nineham and John Fenton. If I have inadvertently offered another's insight as my own, I offer my apologies. To both I offer my thanks for their part in my formation.

Peter Sills
St Francis Day, 2005

Introduction

St Mark and his gospel

Despite the familiarity of their names, most of those who wrote the New Testament remain largely unknown men, and this is certainly true of St Mark. His name was John Mark (Acts 15:17); he was a follower of Jesus but not one of the twelve disciples; his mother Mary (one of many Marys in the New Testament) had a house in Jerusalem where the apostles used to meet (Acts 12:12), and after the resurrection he travelled with both St Peter and St Paul. Peter refers to him affectionately as 'Mark, my son' (1 Peter 5:13), and this supports the tradition that his gospel is based on the teaching and memories of St Peter – although this is now questioned. It is the shortest of the four gospels and is generally held to be the first to be written, probably at Rome where St Peter was in prison, around 65 AD. Mark's gospel captures the sense of awe and mystery surrounding the figure of Jesus. The story is told with pace and drama; the controversy caused by the preaching of the gospel is never far away, and everywhere people are 'astounded' at Jesus' words and deeds. This is the way that Mark himself must have experienced Jesus, and his gospel, long neglected by the church, has in recent years come into its own as one of the foundation texts of the New Testament.

Mark's achievement was to pioneer a new literary form. A gospel is not a biography – many of the details about Jesus that we should like to know are just not there; nor is it a complete record of his ministry; as John said, there were many things that Jesus said and did that are not recorded in the gospels (John 20:30); still less is it a text book – systematic statements of the Christian faith came much later. When Mark wrote he had a different purpose in mind; he wrote to evoke faith, again as John said, the gospels were written 'in order that you may believe that Jesus is the Christ, the Son of God, and that through this faith you may have life by his name.' (John 20:31) Mark was a born storyteller and his gospel is full of unforgettable pictures of Jesus. We see Jesus asleep on the 'cushion' in the stern of the fishing boat (4:39), taking little children in the crook of his arm (9:36), striding ahead of the disciples on the road to Jerusalem, a great lonely figure, wholly absorbed in his coming passion (10:32). Jesus is portrayed with great realism: not as some kind of demi-god, but as a real man with real human needs and feelings. He is angry (1:41), dejected (7:34), filled with compassion (6:34), so stricken with deadly sorrow that he cries 'My heart is ready to break with grief' (14:33). Alongside this there is also the aura of the numinous, the charisma of the holy and the imprint of the divine which belongs to this man.

Through the whole of Mark's story runs a mysterious undercurrent, reminding us that this is not just an account of the life and death of the best man that ever lived. Maybe this comes across best in the note of authority – the sense of divine purpose – which informs Jesus' words and claims. At the heart of the mystery is his consciousness of his divine Sonship which flames out at certain moments, e.g. his baptism and his transfiguration. Mark does not let us forget that Jesus had a precious communion and union with the one he called 'Abba', Father, which was the deepest secret of his life and the source of his authority. It was this in the end which meant that the grave could not hold him. As Mark records, he is risen, and the words of the centurion at the foot of the cross express his own faith, 'Truly this man was the Son of God.' (15:39)

Mark drew on other sources as well as the memories of Peter, including his own experience. A notable example of personal experience is his presence at the arrest of Jesus in the Garden of Gethsemane. The passion stories of Mark, Matthew and Luke show marked similarities which point to a common source. Into this common story Mark alone introduces the incident of the young man who fled naked: 'Among those following was a young man with nothing on but a linen cloth. They tried to sieze him; but he slipped out of the linen cloth and ran away naked.' (14:51-52) There is a tradition that identifies that young man as Mark himself, and the inclusion of the story is his way of saying, 'I was there.'

Mark met St Paul when Paul came to Jerusalem with Barnabas. When they returned to Antioch they took Mark with them (Acts 12:15), and he accompanied them on their first missionary journey. From Antioch they travelled to Seleucia, and from there they sailed to Cyprus: 'Arriving at Salamis, they declared the Word of God in the Jewish Synagogues. They went through the whole island as far as Paphos.' (Acts 13:5-6) At Paphos they came across Elymas, the sorcerer, who posed as a prophet and tried to oppose them. But Paul saw through him and struck him blind for a time – a graphic way of demonstrating that the truth was hidden from his eyes. After their journey across Cyprus, Barnabas and Paul sailed to Perga in Pamphylia (now southern Turkey), and Mark returned to Jerusalem. Later he visited Cyprus again as the companion of Barnabas. Some time after their first missionary journey Paul and Barnabas decided to re-visit the towns they had evangelised. However, they disagreed over their travelling companions: 'Barnabas wanted to take John Mark with them; but Paul judged that the man who had deserted them in Pamphylia and had not gone on to share in their work was not the man to take with them now. Their dispute was so sharp that they parted company.' (Acts 15:37-39) In time the breach was healed, and Mark stayed with Paul when he was in Rome in prison. In his letters to the Colossians and to Philemon, both written from Rome, Paul sends greetings from his companions including Mark, whom he tells us was Barnabas' cousin. (Col 4:10)

Virtually nothing is known of Mark apart from the New Testament writings. Eusebius, a first century historian, records that Mark went to Alexandria, one of the main cities of the ancient world. Although it is not mentioned by other writers, including Clement of Alexandria, the tradition persists, and

Mark is reckoned to have been the first Bishop of Alexandria. The Roman World was not a safe place for Christians, and many accepted death rather than forswear Christ and worship the Emperor. Mark is believed to have been among these first martyrs, meeting his death in the eighth year of Nero. It was the willingness of the first Christians to die for their beliefs which was profoundly impressive in the ancient world, where religion often amounted to no more than a formal civic observance. That religion could entail a profound commitment of mind and heart was not merely novel, it also spoke powerfully to the spiritual needs of an age without God and without hope. The faith that led Mark to write his gospel also shaped his life: he died as he lived.

Mark is believed to have been buried in Alexandria, but early in the ninth century his body was brought to Venice, whose patron he became, and has rested there to this day. Although the original church of St Mark there was burned in 976, the rebuilt basilica contains both the relics from Alexandria and the magnificent series of mosaics depicting Mark's life, death and translation.

Using this book

The main part of this book is divided into six chapters, one for each of the six weeks of Lent, including Holy Week. Each chapter has an introduction and six sections, each of which reflects on a part of Mark's gospel. You will also need a copy of the gospel. The text I have used is the Revised English Bible, and this is the version from which the quotations are taken, but any modern translation will do. How you use the book depends on how your week works out, and whether you are doing it alone or with others. If you can read a section each day, then on Sunday you might like to read the whole of the passage of the gospel for the week and the introduction to the chapter; on the succeeding days read the six sections comprising a gospel passage and reflection. At the end of each section there is a suggested spiritual exercise. You may like simply to do the exercise, or to reflect on the gospel passage using *lectio divina* (the method of praying with the Bible described below), or both! If you are reading this book with others in a group, the final section of each chapter concludes with a question or reflection that offers a way into discussion.

Praying with the Bible
For some people the Bible is simply literature – great literature perhaps, but no more authoritative than the other great writings of the world. Although Christians understand the Bible in different ways, some taking a more or less literal approach to the text, others adopting a more critical stance, there is a common conviction that it is more than literature; it is the revealed Word of God, and as such has an authority that transcends other texts. Because it is so important, designed to evoke faith in God, we need both to be clear what it means and to allow its teaching to shape our lives and our outlook on the world, and this of course accounts for the strong differences of opinion about how it should be read. Anything that is really important is bound to cause controversy simply because it makes demands upon us. This book explores some of those demands, and offers a way of allowing them to shape our lives by learning to pray with the Bible.

Again there is no one way of doing this, but a way that I have found helpful is *lectio divina*, sacred reading, sometimes called the Benedictine method because it is the way of praying that St Benedict commended to his monks. The aim of this way of praying is not to seek to understand the text intellectually but rather to let it speak to us intuitively or imaginatively. This is not to criticise intellectual study, but to say that we need to use other faculties in addition to the intellect if we are to appreciate scripture in all its fullness. So Benedict taught his monks first to listen and reflect rather than to think and question. We try to enter into the atmosphere, the shape, the feeling of the text in the same way that we might experience a beautiful garden or a wonderful view. It is the overall effect of the garden or the panorama that first strikes us; we simply look at it, trying to take it all in and imprint it on our memory. Then we might walk round and look at the individual shrubs and flowers.

Before we begin, we need to prepare ourselves and to ask God to be with us as we pray. Decide first roughly how long your time of prayer will be, and don't be too ambitious! Ten or fifteen (or perhaps twenty) minutes would be about right at the outset. Adopt a comfortable but attentive posture, like sitting in a reasonably upright position; recall that you are in the presence of God and offer him your time of prayer, perhaps saying a simple prayer or lighting a candle. For example:

Father, I offer this time to you;
open my ears to hear your word;
let it live in my heart and shape my life,
for Jesus' sake. Amen.

Or, when lighting a candle:

Father, let this light be to me a sign of your great Light;
let it be a light upon my path
guiding me to your holy mountain,
to the place where you dwell. Amen.

Lectio divina has four stages: reading, meditating, praying, and contemplating.

Reading
First read the text slowly, ideally speaking the words quietly to yourself. When a word or phrase arrests your attention, stop.

Meditating
Repeat the word or phrase slowly to yourself – again this is best done orally: meditation is done with the mouth rather than just with the mind. The process is rather like savouring a sweet – one that is so good we want it to last! Or we may liken it to striking a bell and listening to the echoes. When the echoes have died away, repeat the word or phrase again, or perhaps just part of the phrase, or a single word. Just as we gradually absorb the sweet or let the tones of the bell touch our depths, so we gradually absorb

the text and let it become part of us. When this process seems to have reached a natural conclusion, offer a brief prayer.

Praying

Prayer, said St Benedict, should be brief. Perhaps some new insight has occurred to you: say thank you to God, simply and directly, and ask him to help you to learn from it. Perhaps you have been reminded of someone or something: pray for them / it briefly. Perhaps you have become aware of where you fall short, or of something that you should do: ask God to heal you or to enable you to do what you need to do. Whatever your prayer, it should arise out of the scripture. Then rest.

Contemplating

The final stage is contemplation. Mother Mary Clare, one of the Sisters of the Love of God, described contemplation as 'basically a looking towards God ... It is not having nice or pretty thoughts; it is not having a sensible realisation of his presence. It is the return of the whole being back to God, more often than not in the darkness of faith and in increasing dependency on the spirit of God in prayer.' (Mother Mary Clare, SLG, *Encountering the Depths*, p 3) In contemplation mental activity is superseded, and all we are aware of is presence. It is a state known to lovers in the presence of their beloved; all they can do is to look and behold. Contemplation is resting in a wordless communion with God. This often takes time to experience, and I met one Benedictine monk who said he did not think he had ever achieved it! It is, I think, something given rather than attained. The important thing is to pause and, as far as you can, to hold the whole experience before God. It is rather like a long pause before the applause at the end of a concert in which the whole experience of the music is present. This too will reach a natural conclusion, and when you are ready pick up the text and continue reading until another word or phrase leaps off the page.

Clearly this way of reading the Bible takes time – it took me a year to read St Mark's gospel in this way! But it has value whether or not you use it to read the whole of the text or just to reflect on the part of the passage for the day.

I

Proclaiming the Kingdom
Chapters 1-3

Introduction

Mark begins his gospel as he means to go on. Unlike the other gospels there is no account of Jesus' birth, no shepherds, no wise men, no table of his descent, no philosophical prologue; Mark begins simply and directly: 'The beginning of the gospel of Jesus Christ the Son of God.'

After the briefest of introductions – just fourteen verses – recording the ministry of John the Baptist in Judea, Mark immediately takes us north, and tells us that after John had been arrested, Jesus came into Galilee proclaiming the gospel of God: 'The time has come; the kingdom of God is upon you; repent and believe the gospel.' Here, in a few words, Mark sets out the whole theme of Jesus' ministry. The time all Israel has been waiting for has come; the new age has dawned; the age long foretold by the prophets when God would come among his people has broken into history. After this astounding claim, the story moves at great pace, as if to emphasise the urgency of the task that Jesus faced. The first disciples are called; many people are healed, including a man with an unclean spirit; the people are taught – and are astounded at the authority with which Jesus speaks. Despite pleas to stay in Capernaum, Jesus insists that he must move on to the other towns and, Mark tells us, he makes a journey around the whole of Galilee – and we have not yet reached the end of chapter one!

When Jesus returns to Capernaum, Mark introduces the theme that will run throughout his gospel, the conflict between Jesus and the religious authorities. The occasion is the healing of the paralysed man who is let down by his friends through the roof of the house where Jesus was staying. The healing is cou-

16

pled with the forgiveness of the man's sins. To the religious lawyers in the crowd this is blasphemy; 'Who but God alone can forgive sins?' they cry out. The matter is made worse when Jesus eats with tax-gatherers and other bad characters; to the Pharisees' protest he replies: 'It is not the healthy that need a doctor, but the sick; I did not come to invite virtuous people, but sinners.'

The teaching, the power to forgive sins, and the power over the unclean spirits, all demonstrate Jesus' authority. Mark is clear: the new age has dawned with Jesus; it will bring hope for those who acknowledge their sins, but it will bring judgement for those who do not. Jesus is a healer, but he is also divisive – in the sense that the truth is divisive. The truth shows up those who are in error, just as light shows up those who hide in the darkness. Jesus' very presence cannot be other than a source of division in a world where error and darkness prevail. The coming of Jesus divides people into two groups: those who are for him and those who are against him, and it is clear by the beginning of chapter three who those two groups are. The ordinary people give praise to God saying, 'Never before have we seen the like.' But when Jesus challenges the sabbath laws by healing the man with the withered arm, 'the Pharisees began plotting against him with the men of Herod's party to bring about Jesus' death.' The chapter ends with a shocking example of the divisions that Jesus will bring. His family come to take charge of him, for the people were saying that he was out of his mind, but their care is rejected: 'Who is my mother? Who are my brothers?' Jesus asks, and looking at those around him, he says: 'Here are my mother and my brothers. Whoever does the will of God is my brother, my sister, and my mother.' It is not the natural ties of the family that save us, but our allegiance to Jesus.

This is disturbing stuff, and we ought to find it disturbing. Mark wants to disturb us into understanding the truth about Jesus, just as Jesus disturbed his hearers into realising what the time to which they had looked forward really meant. The urgency, the drama, the confrontation, the demand for allegiance, all emphasise the radical difference between the old and the new. 'No one puts new wine into old wineskins; if he does the wine will burst the skins, and then wine and skins are both lost. Fresh skins for new wine!'

1. Prepare the Way
Read Mark 1:1-20

The time has come; the scriptures are fulfilled! In Jesus' day it was believed that the coming of the Messiah would be heralded by the return of Elijah, the first of the great prophets. Mark makes it clear that this belief was fulfilled by the appearance of John the Baptist. He begins his account of John's ministry with the words of Isaiah, 'I am sending my herald ahead of you; he will prepare your way.' It is not without significance that John appeared in the wilderness, away from the capital. I think of a wilderness rather like a garden that has grown wild, but on a huge scale; a disorienting place where it is easy to get lost, a fearful place where trees and creepers close in menacingly and its sounds induce panic. Maybe the Judean wilderness was once like that, but today it is a rocky wasteland, a waterless place where only a few scrubby plants can survive. But in these barren wastes it is easy to get lost, and if you walk it alone it is not long before disorientation and panic take hold. Either way the wilderness symbolises fear and confusion, the loss of direction and purpose in life. It was to such a place that John called the people: Are your lives confused? Have you lost your way? Does God seem far away? Take heart, there is a way back. Even here in this place you can be washed clean, and there is One who is coming who will lead you back to God. I baptise you with water; he will baptise you with the Holy Spirit.

Feeling confused about life, seeking a way out of the wilderness, is familiar enough; it is part of being human. Sometimes things just overwhelm us and we break down; more often the sheer routine of living saps our energies and dulls our sense of purpose. Lent is a time to regain energy and re-connect with our purpose in life. Losing our way, missing the mark is essentially what sin is about. Sin is more a state of being than a series of wrongful acts or omissions. Most people are not sinners in the sense of leading corrupt and wicked lives; but we are all sinners in the sense that our lives are not as focused on God as they should be. We have missed the mark like an arrow that is off target. So when John baptised those who came to him confessing their sins I doubt if he was dealing with the notorious wrongdoers of Jerusalem. More likely those who came were ordinary people who felt that their lives were off target, and who were seeking a new direction. Going to the wilderness symbolised both their sense of lostness, and their need to let go of the familiar in order to sort themselves out. Gaining a true sense of perspective meant distancing themselves from all the concerns that beset their everyday lives.

Lent with its discipline of giving things up and giving more time to prayer and good works has the same purpose. It is meant to distance ourselves a bit from our everyday concerns so that we can get a better perspective on our lives. We are all a bit wide of the mark; we are all in need of the renewing grace and for-giveness of God if we are going to get ourselves back on track. That gift was given when we were baptised; Lent is the time to renew it, to hear the voice of Jesus saying, 'Take heart, there is a way back. I will wash you clean and guide you in my way. Fear no more, for you are mine and I have redeemed you.'

As you reflect on John the Baptist's ministry, imagine your-self telling John about those parts of your life that feel confused, lost or afraid. Speak to him about your desire for God to come close and lead you home, and feel the renewing waters as he pours them over you.

2. Repent and Believe
Read Mark 1:14-45

Jesus' ministry was essentially a call to repentance. Mark sum-marises it neatly: 'After John had been arrested, Jesus came into Galilee proclaiming the gospel of God: "The time has come: the kingdom of God is upon you. Repent and believe the good news".' 'Repent' is a strong word. It is not the same as feeling sorry or regretful, or even being contrite; it is about making a deep inner change. To repent is to turn, to face in a new direction; repentance is an act of the will: a deep desire to change, to face a new way, to take a new direction in life – and taking steps to put this desire into effect. Feeling sorry can be the beginning of repentance, especially if it brings with it a desire to make amends. God certainly wants us to feel sorry that we have missed the mark, but he wants more than sorrow; he wants us to change and focus our lives on Jesus. This essentially is what we try to do in Lent. Lent is about turning, changing direction, bringing our lives around, bit by bit, so that we are more and more focused on Jesus.

'Repent and believe ...' I wonder if anyone asked 'Why?' 'Why should I repent and believe? What has this good news to do with me?' In reply Jesus might have posed another question: 'Deep down are you happy with your life? Do you feel connected with what's real and gives life meaning? Is your spirit really alive?' Jesus came to set people free so that they might have life in all its fullness, to use St John's phrase. (John 10:10) Why should I repent and believe? Because that is the path to life; that is the way you will find out who you truly are; that is the way you will find peace for your soul. St Benedict said the same to his monks: ' "Who desires life and is eager to see good days?" If you hear this and reply, "I do", God says to you, "If you want true and everlasting life turn from evil and do good; seek peace and follow after it".' (*Rule of St Benedict*, Prologue 15-17)

The good news, the gospel that Jesus proclaimed, was that through him a new start was possible. Mark illustrates this in two ways. First he describes Jesus calling Simon and Andrew, and James and John to follow him. They did so and began a new life in which they discovered not only who Jesus was but also who they were themselves. Second Mark describes the impact Jesus had on the people of Capernaum. He taught them and they were amazed; he healed them and they were astounded. Mark tells us that it was his 'authority' that marked Jesus out from the other teachers and healers of his day. His authority knew no bounds: 'When he gives orders,' the people exclaimed, 'even the unclean spirits obey.' The teaching and the healing went together: he spoke of new life and by his actions he gave new life; his acts showed that his words were true – no wonder the whole town gathered at his door. But despite so many coming to be cured Jesus moved on around the whole of Galilee. Mark brings out clearly the imperative to move: it is the message that is vital (literally 'life-giving'), not the cures. When his companions asked him to remain in Capernaum, Jesus responded: 'Let us move on to the neighbouring towns, so that I can proclaim my message there as well, for that is what I came to do.'

Lents come and go. Why do we observe these forty days before Easter? Why do we give things up, like sweets or alcohol, or make a special collection for those in need? What has this got to do with the rest of my life? Maybe we wonder why our past Lents, so full of good resolutions and pious practices, seem to have borne so little fruit. The answer may be that we have done these things without relating them to the supreme end of our lives, our relationship with God. Or, to put it another way, do we really want to hear the message that Jesus proclaimed? Turning and facing a new way is not easy, and we really need to be convinced that it will be worth the effort. So, as we set out on this Lent perhaps we should ask how it will relate to our need for inner peace, to our search for our true selves, to our desire to have life in all its fullness. Bede Frost in his book, *Lent with St Benedict*, says, 'Lent is [not a] time to decorate ourselves with pious exercises, but one for securing and strengthening the foundations of the spiritual life.' Perhaps we do see Lent in that way, but inner peace is still hard to come by. If so, we might probe a little deeper and ask how our spiritual life relates to the rest of our lives? Do we live an integrated life?

Taking Jesus as our focus we can see what an integrated life looks like. Not for him living in separate compartments: God on Sunday, work on Monday, with different values and attitudes for each. Mark records briefly that after his baptism Jesus with-

drew to the wilderness for forty days where he was tempted by
Satan. This time of testing gave him a deep determination to put
God first, and these forty days of Lent are given to us to for the
same purpose: to help us put God first, to turn around, in a
word, to repent. It is by getting our priorities right that we bring
balance to our lives and integrate our faith with our work in the
world.

As you reflect today ask yourself: How much do I want to
hear Jesus' good news?

3. Blasphemous Healing
Read Mark 2:1-17

It is evident from the little that Mark has told us so far that Jesus
is an unsettling figure. He will not be confined by people's expectations, even by their need for healing; proclaiming his message is his overriding priority. With the story of the healing of
the paralysed man, Mark makes plain the price that he will pay
for proclaiming that message. The story also reveals more fully
who Jesus is: his power to heal the body is a sign that he can
make us completely whole – at one with God – and that is what
forgiveness achieves.

The scandal of the healing in the eyes of the religious establishment, here represented by the scribes, is not the cure but the
authority asserted in performing it. The setting is dramatic.
There is a huge crowd over-spilling the space in front of the
house; there are the four friends who, despite the crowd, found
a way of bringing their paralysed companion to Jesus; and there
are the scribes, sitting apart. Like the crowd the scribes are
drawn to Jesus, but at the same time they have come to check up
on him. Jesus seems to use the occasion in a quite deliberate way
to challenge them, for he knows what they are there for. And so
the drama unfolds. As Jesus talks the friends make an opening
in the roof and lower the sick man on his bed to the ground.
Mark records that when Jesus saw the faith of the friends he said
to the paralysed man, 'My son, your sins are forgiven.' Jesus
must have known that this would shock the scribes, for only

God could forgive sins. So in a dramatic demonstration of his authority to forgive sins, Jesus turns to the paralysed man and says, 'I say to you, stand up, take your bed and go home.' The cure is instantaneous, and the man gets up, takes up his bed and goes home. I can imagine an awed silence descending upon the crowd as they part to let the man through, and then, as they watch him go, breaking out in astonishment: 'Never before have we seen anything like this.'

The response of the three groups is instructive. The crowd are in no doubt that they have witnessed God in action, for they praise him: not only was the man healed, he is forgiven. But it is not clear that they equate Jesus with God; I doubt if they did. It would have been the healing rather than the claim to be able to forgive sins that made the deepest impression. But this is precisely what the scribes, the trained professionals, noticed. They too must have been impressed by the healing, but the divine claim of which it was an eloquent sign was blasphemous, and this was deeply shocking. Jesus could not be allowed to claim that he acted with the authority of God, and if he did he must be punished.

The response of the four friends is not recorded. Perhaps they were simply grateful that their brother could now walk; perhaps they shared the general feeling of the crowd. It is the faith of the friends that Mark records, and their persistence in bringing the sick man to Jesus. Perhaps they had grasped the truth, or at least an inkling of it, that Jesus was in fact the Son of God. Had not the prophets foretold that God would come among them and offer a new beginning to his people bearing their infirmities and forgiving their sins? Who, having seen his deeds, could doubt that Jesus was the One who was to come, as John the Baptist had proclaimed, whatever the scribes might think?

Forgiveness lies at the heart of the good news that Jesus came to proclaim. God, he told his hearers, is like a loving father who longs for his people to be reconciled to him. A new beginning was a possibility for everyone, not just for those who kept all the demands of the Law without fault. This message was heard by the people gladly, like those crowding around him when the paralysed man was brought to him; and it was this message that drove Jesus to tour the whole district of Galilee. God's priority was and is the lost and the outcast. Mark makes this plain in a second story about a meal that Jesus shared with 'many tax collectors and sinners'. Again the story is based on a contrast between different groups of people, in this case the guests around the table with Jesus, and the scribes on the outside who observed what was going on. This time their criticism is voiced rather than silent: they say to their disciples, 'Why does he eat with tax collectors and sinners?' Jesus overhears them, as perhaps he was intended to do, and responds, 'It is not the healthy that need a doctor, but the sick. I did not come to call the virtuous but sinners.'

People who are doing their best to live a Christian life can feel a bit discouraged by this. Is God really interested in us? Where do we come in his priorities? The answer to this is given by St Luke in the parable of the lost son. (Luke 15:11-32) God has a special place in his heart for those who are already with him; he rejoices over the righteous. But being on God's side and living a prayerful and moral life does not entitle us to divine favours. If the godly are truly close to God then they will share his concern for those who are not; if they don't (like the elder son in the parable) then they need to ask just what their closeness amounts to in practice. This is the challenge that Jesus puts to the scribes: You have kept all the rules and said your prayers, but has that brought you close to God? Have you really grasped what God is about? Knowledge about God is not the same as knowing God; keeping the rules is not the same as righteousness.

As you reflect on these two stories, ask yourself where you place yourself: with the crowd, the scribes, or the friends? Ask Jesus to help you move closer to him.

4. Lord of the Sabbath

Read Mark 2:18-3:19a

Jesus clearly aroused a wide range of feelings among the people, from curiosity to suspicion and enmity. One reason for this was that he seemed to sit light to the law and customs that regulated everyday life, especially religious life. Mark gives three examples in this section: Jesus feasts when others fast, and he works on the sabbath, gathering food and healing the sick. But clearly he was not a rebel, throwing over the accepted ways and preaching a religious and moral permissiveness. He was totally serious about God; his healing miracles could not be dismissed, and they authenticated his claim to speak and act with God's authority. His response to those who criticised him for not observing a fast like the disciples of John the Baptist and the Pharisees made no concessions to his critics. His disciples must celebrate the time that he is with them, he said, just as they would at a wedding; celebration is the only response to being in the presence of God. (The radical nature of his new way is shown in his sayings about the coat and the wine; he offers not only new wine, but also a new vessel to contain it.) However, Jesus adds a warning: he will not be with them for ever; when he is gone it will be time for his followers to fast. Even at this early stage in his story Mark lets his reader know how it will end; the signs of conflict are not just about trivial rules but about a struggle that goes to the heart of the Jewish understanding of God and what it means to worship him. Even now Jesus is aware that he will pay for his challenge with his death. That this is no empty threat Mark makes apparent at the end of this section. As the Pharisees leave the synagogue where the man with the withered arm has been healed 'at once [they] began plotting with the men of Herod's party to bring about Jesus' death.'

The essence of Jesus' challenge is summed-up in his pithy saying, 'The sabbath was made for man, not man for the sabbath: so the Son of Man is Lord even of the sabbath.' It is perhaps difficult for us to enter into the shock that this would have produced in a pious Jew, and even in a not-too-pious Jew. Sabbath

observance was one of the pillars of the Law, and people measured their righteousness according to the strictness with which
they kept its rules. It must have seemed to many that the sabbath
came first, like a god who must be obeyed. Jesus turns this on its
head. The sabbath rules were a means of helping people to come
close to God, they were not an end in themselves. If they became
an end in themselves, taking people away from God, then they
could be ignored.

A good parallel is in the way we observe Lent. There are four
traditional lenten disciplines: fasting, almsgiving, study and
prayer. These can be undertaken in a more or less automatic
way, as ends in themselves – the things we always do in Lent –
without thinking too much about their deeper purpose. They are
meant to be practical ways of building deeper foundations for
our spiritual lives. We fast to discipline our bodily appetites –
and not just for food. What we want so easily becomes an object
of desire, of consuming passion, in a word, of worship. So we go
without not to help us slim, or to cure a bad habit, but to remind
ourselves of our inner emptiness that only God can fill. Each
time we refuse a drink or chocolate or whatever, is a reminder
that we cannot live by bread alone, but only by the word of God.
We may give alms to help the needy or ease our conscience, but
if that is all we miss the point. Almsgiving is a reminder that our
worth is not measured by our wealth, but by our love. Each
pound or penny we put aside for the poor reminds us that no
man is an island; God's special concern is for the poor, and our
eternal destiny is inseparable from theirs. We may study to increase our knowledge or our usefulness, or just because we like
reading books, but study is not about self-improvement. We
study so that the Word may dwell in our hearts. God has called
us to be his witnesses; he expects us to be able to give a reason
for the faith that is in us. Each book we read or course we attend
is a reminder that God's word is the source of life. Prayer is the
way we tune in to God, the way we get on to his wavelength. We
pray because God made us to pray, because he wants to commu-
nicate with each of us personally. We may want God to do

something for others, but we pray first and foremost because God wants to draw us close to him and enfold us in his love. Every prayer we make is a reminder that God is love; he is to be trusted not tested.

The man with the withered arm is a symbol of the deadening effect of wrong religion, taking away life rather than giving it; incapacitating rather than enabling. In healing him with the simple command 'Stretch out your arm', Jesus shows the power of his Way to bring wholeness. This, says the Lord of the Sabbath, is what God desires, that his people should be whole, able to reach out to him with their whole being.

Reflect on what you are doing for Lent: Why, for example, are you reading this book? Ask God to help your lenten discipline become a way to new life, a taste of his new wine: Lord, where do I need healing? Help me stretch out my arm to you.

5. Kith and Kin
Read Mark 3:19b-35

After recording another astonishing incident in Jesus' ministry, where 'great numbers' of people from the whole of the northern part of Israel came to be healed, and the calling of the twelve, Mark introduces Jesus' family into the story. The contrast with St Luke's account of the holy family is marked. Mark has no birth or infancy stories, with Mary treasuring the sayings of angels and saints in her heart (Luke 2:19 & 51). His first mention of the family is when they come to take charge of Jesus because they think he is 'out of his mind'. (Luke does record this incident, but makes nothing of it: Luke 8:19-21.) We have here an account of two encounters, one with the family and the other with the teachers of the law who had come down from Jerusalem. Jesus had much in common with both; he had a common blood relationship with his family, and with the teachers of the law he had a common calling, but in each case they had chosen different paths. The differences between those who ought to be close but who see things differently are usually very marked and can be bitter, as we may know from experience of families who fall out, and of professional jealousy. The story of Jesus and his family is in two parts and presumably Mark places the story about the dispute with the rabbis between them because he means us to understand the one in relation to the other.

As we have seen, the rabbis were impressed by Jesus' healing powers, so much so that they saw him as a threat, and so they set out to discredit him. They say that his power comes from Beelzebul. It is a cheap gibe that Jesus easily refutes: a house divided against itself, he says, cannot stand. Satan cannot drive himself out. I imagine that the Rabbis were not persuaded. They probably went away indignant that an unlearned carpenter should give them lessons! He ought to go to college and study the subject properly. There is probably more than a hint of snobbery here. Jesus was a northerner, a Galilean who spoke with a regional accent. The rabbis were from the capital in the south, sophisticated and erudite. It was unthinkable that God had sent someone from the rough, unsophisticated north to teach them. How often it is that the sophisticated assume that the simple have nothing to offer them! Jesus' simplicity was that of one who had seen through the complexities to the real truth, and this was where his note of authority came from. I used to be a lawyer and remember being impressed by some words of Lord Radcliffe, one of the most distinguished lawyers of his generation, who said that he felt that the law had become too complex and could not bear the weight of learning that was expended upon it. Complexity and subtlety of distinction had made the law too remote. Jesus was saying the same thing about religion; it had become too complex, with all its subtle and complicated rules about sabbath observance, for example; only the 'professional religious' like the Pharisees could keep it. In place of the mountain of rules Jesus offered two simple precepts: love God, and love your neighbour as yourself. Love is shown in self-sacrifice not in self-assertion.

The tragedy of Israel, Mark suggests, is the tragedy of a divided family, with all the problems that brings about identity and security. When a family splits the question arises as to who is the real family, and some will try to bring the errant into line. According to Mark, Mary does not appear to have understood what Jesus was really about. Maybe she hoped, like any parent, that he would turn out alright and follow the family line. For a time he did, but when he turned away from it she and the rest of the family assumed that he was out of his mind. 'Our family don't do these things', or as Lady Thatcher put it, 'He's not one of us.' The rabbis responded the same way. By discrediting those who are different (or saying they are mad) we avoid listening to what they have to say. Christians (and Anglicans in particular) do this to each other all the time; small differences, if unhealed, lead to major feuds and bloody separations. What is the word that God speaks to those brothers and sisters who are estranged? It is the answer that Jesus gave to those who told him that his family was at the door, 'Whoever does the will of God is my brother and sister and mother.' In the church as in other areas of life, Jesus' words require us to accept the sincerity and motivation of those who seek to do God's will but who do not seem to be like us and with whom we find it hard to make common cause. Denying the work of the Spirit in their lives is the one thing that Jesus says will not be forgiven. More fundamental than our blood relationships, our fellowship in a common calling or our shared social standing, is our relationship to Jesus.

Think today about your family and those with whom you work and worship. Are there relationships that need to be healed, people whom you find hard to accept as honestly and sincerely motivated? Ask God to help you see things as they see them.

6. Kairos and Chronos

'The time has come ...' Jesus began his ministry with an urgent call to repentance. He challenges us to turn around our whole being, changing the way we face, changing our priorities, and putting God first.

'The time has come ...' The Greeks have two words for time: *chronos* meaning clock time, and *kairos* meaning significant time, a time of destiny or of fulfilment or of reckoning. The coming of Jesus was not just a moment in time, but a *kairos* moment, like a declaration of love, or of war, a time in which things are revealed as they truly are. He challenged people to recognise that in him God had fulfilled his promise that he would come among his people and set them free, forgiving their sins and making a new relationship with God possible. Times of destiny and judgement are disturbing; loyalties and allegiances are made plain.

'The time has come ...' Jesus came from the wilderness having done battle with the devil, rejecting his temptations to conform to the way of the world. To celebrate Lent is to make a wilderness journey. A time to step back and reflect, to hear again the call of Jesus in our own ears: 'The kingdom of God is upon you; repent and believe the gospel.' Lent is a time to seek healing, especially inner healing and the healing of relationships. We no longer speak of demons, but they are still there, manifesting themselves in the spirit of the age with its shallow relationships, designer morality, and with a price on everything. Lent is a time to sharpen our senses, especially our sense of time. We are so driven by *chronos* that we are deaf to *kairos*. We need to quicken our sense of urgency in the task that faces us, both personally and communally.

Personally, there will be a time when we stand before God and give an account of our stewardship. One of the subtlest temptations is to think that we can sort out our lives later, a task for retirement, perhaps. Now I have got to live in the real world, and that means a bit of flexibility; I'll have more time for God later. But are we earning a living or making a life? They have to go hand in hand; the longer you leave it the harder it gets. The time has come: do it now.

Communally, we live in a world that believes it can do without God. The opening years of the third millennium have dashed the hopes with which it started. A few names make the point: Enron, Al Quaeda, Twin Towers, Iraq, Darfur, Tsunami, Gleneagles, Katrina. If we do not see them as signs of a *kairos* moment, then we have not really seen them. In the face of terrorism, trade injustice, natural disasters and corporate wickedness we look for military, political, economic and technological solutions and ignore the spiritual malaise that allows greed, violence and injustice to breed. The time has come; we have to act now before it is too late.

Jesus' mission was to Israel whom God had called to be his people. They were to be a sign to the world of his righteousness, his justice and his peace. It is easy to forget that the church is the new Israel, the new People of God, whom Jesus described as the salt which leavens the whole. Sorting out our lives is part of the process by which we serve the world. The more open we are to God, the deeper will be our commitment to him, and the more we can be used by him in the world. The time has come; surely, we need no convincing of the urgency of this task.

II

In Deed and Word
Chapters 4-6

Introduction

Mark moves from his most dramatic opening to a collection of stories about Jesus' parables and miracles which drive home his basic message that Jesus is God's new beginning; in him the true New Age has dawned. The three parables are about growth: the Sower, the Seed Growing Secretly, and the Mustard Seed, and in each the emphasis is on the power of God to bring much out of a little. This is profoundly reassuring. We may feel hopeless in the face of the challenge that Jesus puts before us, both in the world and in our personal lives, but Mark reminds us that God does not ask us to undertake a task without giving us the tools to do the job. The important lesson of these stories is that God is the real agent of change; in his hands our little becomes much.

These parables are followed by the accounts of four miracles: Jesus calms the storm, heals the Gerasene demoniac, and the woman with haemorrhages, and raises Jairus' daughter. Miracles are not just amazing events, they are signs which point beyond the deed itself to a greater truth or reality. Mark has more miracle stories per page than the other gospels; eighteen in all. By telling these stories Mark encourages us to see in Jesus the same power at work through which the world was created, and which is now at work again to re-create it, heal it and to bring it new life. By calming the storm Jesus shows the same power over nature that inheres in God. No wonder the disciples were awe-struck: 'Who can this be,' they said to one another, 'even the wind and the sea obey him?' The two healing miracles are both about wholeness: to the demoniac Jesus brings wholeness of mind, to the woman wholeness of body. And we should not overlook the fact that for both of them wholeness brings freedom; they are released from bondage into a new fullness of life. These three miracles are powerful signs of the extent of Jesus' authority, but its full extent is shown in the fourth. When he raises Jairus' daughter, Jesus shows that his power extends to the final enemy, death itself, the event which was thought to separate man from God. As St Paul came to understand, there is nothing that can separate us from the love of God in Christ, nothing, not even death. (Romans 8:35-39)

This section ends with a reflection on discipleship. Jesus has not come as a lone figure, intruding briefly upon the world to bring comfort to a few and to amaze us by his words and miracles. He has come as the sign and agent of God who is always present in the world and who, in Jesus, offers us a new beginning; what God does through him he will also do through those who put their trust in him. So, very soon after they have been called Jesus sends out the twelve 'two by two with authority over unclean spirits'. Their mission is successful: 'they drove out many demons, and anointed many sick people with oil and cured them,' and on their return they reported to Jesus 'all that they had done and taught'. Around this story of success Mark places two other stories that illustrate the cost that this discipleship carries. The first is the death of John the Baptist. What Jesus does and says may impress the powerful, but it also challenges them, and in the end worldly concerns may weigh more in their hearts than their concern for truth and holiness. In doing the work of God the disciples put their own lives at risk. The second story is about the feeding of the five thousand and the sequel of Jesus walking on the lake. When Jesus again calms the wind, Mark records that the disciples 'were utterly astounded, for they had not understood the incident of the loaves; their minds were closed'. It not enough for Jesus' followers to heal and teach in his name; if they are to understand the true significance of what they do they must let their own minds and hearts be changed. Then, as now, people often begin to follow Jesus because he has warmed their hearts. A warm heart gives confidence and strength, and God will use it to bring comfort and healing to others, but a warmed heart is not automatically a changed heart. The warming can be experienced as confirmation that our outlook on life – and on God – is correct. Generally this is not the case. Our outlook on life and our ideas about God have been formed by years of immersion in a particular family, society, economic and political system, and as Mark makes plain throughout his gospel – and indeed has just illustrated in the story of King Herod and John the Baptist – there is generally some slippage between this acquired outlook and the teaching of Jesus. It takes time to change attitudes so deeply formed, whatever the outward signs may be. The disciples rejoiced in what God had done through them, and rightly; but even so, says Mark, they had not understood the true significance of who Jesus was and what he was about. God wants our minds and our morals as well as our hearts. To be a true disciple a warm heart is not enough.

1. Seeds of New Life
Read Mark 4:1-33
Mark does not record as much of the teaching of Jesus as Matthew and Luke, and these three parables, together with the parables in chapters 12 and 13, are the nearest we get to systematic teaching in his gospel. A parable is a word-picture, a true-to-life story that points beyond the everyday situation it describes. Some seem to have been inspired by actual events. A parable is not an allegory, that is, a puzzle whose meaning is discovered by understanding the symbolic significance of each detail of the story. To understand an allegory you have to know the hidden key; to understand a parable you have to let it stimulate your imagination to see the familiar in a new way. So when Jesus wants to teach people about the power of God to transform their lives he uses a familiar situation from everyday life, the farmer sowing seed. However, as recorded by Mark, the parable of the Sower suffers from being accompanied by an explanation that turns it into an allegory. It is unlikely that the explanation goes back to Jesus. Parables were a common form of rabbinic teach-

ing. A parable works on the 'penny dropping' basis; it requires
the hearers to work out the message for themselves, and challenges them to see the world in the same way. No rabbi would
have explained a parable; to do so is like explaining a joke – it
loses its effect. You either see what the parable is about or you
don't; the penny drops or it doesn't. This is not to deny that the
explanation has value: it is a challenge to personal change so
that we become fruitful in God's service, but that is not the real
point of the parable. Looking at the parable without the explanation we see a wonderful picture of God's grace. Sowing seed and
waiting for the harvest was a familiar experience for Jesus' hearers. They knew how their best efforts could be thwarted by the
weather, weeds and birds, and sometimes at the harvest there
would be so little to show for all their hard work that they
would be close to despair. In the parable the harvest exceeds all
expectations despite the problems. This, too, would have been
part of the experience of the audience. The message is clear,
God's harvest exceeds all our expectations – despite the problems and despite those who work against him.

A similar message is contained in the other two parables.
Once planted the seed grows secretly. It contains in itself all that
it needs to grow and bring forth a crop. All that we need to do is
to plant it and care for it so that it can grow: God gives the increase. In the same way people have within them the capacity to
grow into what God has made them to become. As someone
once said, we are hard-wired for God. We must be concerned to
plant the seed of faith, and to provide the conditions in which it
will grow, but thereafter it is God who gives the increase. And
we are not to be concerned about the size of the seed we sow.
Even from the smallest of seeds like the mustard seed, God can
produce a full-grown plant, like a mustard tree – big enough for
birds to shelter in its branches. This is a timely message for a
world and a church which tries to do too much by its own efforts. Keeping the religious rules, like the Pharisees, will not of
itself get us to heaven, nor will self-help, or competition, or the
free market. It is God alone who will get us to heaven. By telling

these stories Mark reminds us that our Lenten journey is about letting go and letting God.

What then of the puzzling passage between the parable and the explanation in which Jesus seems to say that he uses parables to keep his message hidden? (Indeed taking this literally would account for the explanation: it reveals the hidden message!) These verses refer to the call of Isaiah, where the prophet is told: 'Go, tell this people: however hard you listen you will never understand. However hard you look you will never perceive. This people's wits are dulled; they have stopped their ears and shut their eyes, so that they may not see with their eyes, nor listen with their ears, nor understand with their wits, and turn and be healed.' (Isaiah 6:9, 10) God warns Isaiah that his message will not be well received; although he must speak, his words will only serve to confirm his hearers in their human wisdom and to strengthen their resolve to continue in their human ways. In much the same way, Jesus is warning his disciples that although many will listen to their words few will really hear them and allow their hearts to be changed. It is, of course, absurd to suppose that Jesus meant to keep his message hidden; that would frustrate the whole purpose of his coming among us. But the truth has to be discovered, and not simply learnt. Parents and teachers know this: you can tell children endlessly that fire is dangerous, but until they have tried to touch it the warning means little. It's the same with religious truth: to really mean something it has to become part of our experience. And that's what a parable is designed to do: when the penny drops you have made a discovery. Jesus is warning his disciples that many will be fascinated by what they say, but few will let the truth touch them.

In the same way we have a choice about how we hear scripture. Do we come to the Bible looking for comfort or for a challenge? Does the familiarity of the stories dull their edge? We all have certain acquired ideas and our faith is affected by worldly wisdom: How open are we to new meanings? The problem with the explanation of the parable of the Sower is that having read it we think we know what the parable means, and this closes off the possibility of seeing new meanings. Some commentators have suggested it was added to bring encouragement to early Christians suffering persecution, but for most of us the times of persecution have passed, and there is the danger that we read it simply as an encouragement to try to be God's good soil without much in our lives really changing. The original meaning (as suggested above) is more challenging. As you reflect try to put aside the familiar explanation and put yourself into the shoes of those who heard Jesus tell the parable. Can you place yourself in the picture and see what he meant? He said, 'If you have ears to hear, then hear.' You have listened to the words, ask him to help you to be open to hear what he said.

2. Deeds of Power
Read Mark 4:35-5:20
Mark now illustrates the teaching of the parables with four stories about the power of God to bring new life: the calming of the storm, the healing of the demoniac, the healing of the woman with haemorrhages and the raising of Jairus' daughter. He began by saying that Jesus was the Son of God; these stories point to that truth. This section reflects on the first two of those stories, which show the power of God to bring order out of chaos.

The story of Jesus calming the storm points back to the first creation story in which the earth is described as 'a vast waste [and] darkness covered the deep.' (Genesis 1:2) Over this wasteland the Spirit of God hovered and brought forth life. There was an ancient belief, shared at one time by the Jews, that the original act of creation involved a contest between God and the forces of chaos and evil, and this contest was located, so to speak, in the waters of the sea. In consequence ability to control the sea was regarded as a sign of divine power. This belief is reflected in some of the Psalms, for example: 'You rule the raging of the sea, calming the turmoil of its waves.' (Psalm 89:9) Faith that God would save him in the midst of a storm was a sign of the righteous man's complete confidence in God. (St Paul showed this confidence in his journey to Rome when he was shipwrecked: Acts 27:27-end.) By calming the storm – and later by walking on the water – Jesus demonstrates not only the faith of the truly righteous man, but also that the power of God in creation is also at work in him. Out of disorder he brings calm, just as the Word of God in creation brought order out of chaos.

Similarly, in the second story order is brought to the life of a severely disturbed man. We would probably say today that he was suffering from a mental illness or disorder. The description of him as possessed by many demons brings to mind some of the patients I encountered when I did a placement at a psychiatric hospital, people who seemed torn apart by forces within them that were beyond control. Jesus, as a man of his times, naturally believes that Legion's condition is caused by demon possession and exorcises him. The severity of the man's inner chaos, indicated by his name 'Legion', meant that he was in the grip of a great power of evil but, Mark tells us, the power of Jesus was greater. That Jesus had truly cast out so many demons is shown by the drowning of the herd of pigs, an awesome, if extraordinary, confirmation of the miracle. We might give a different explanation today of Legion's condition (understanding the true cause of illness is, perhaps, one area where Jesus' promise that the Holy Spirit would lead us into the truth has been fulfilled: John 16:13), but this is not to deny the power of God to re-order people's lives and to bring healing even in the most difficult situations. Nor is it to deny that something quite remarkable happened to Legion. The story of the pigs rushing into the lake raises disturbing (and unanswerable) questions, but it is unlikely that Mark would have invented something so astonishing; and the response of the swineherds and the townsfolk who 'begged Jesus to leave the district', has the ring of truth.

Some Christians believe in demonic possession – in fact some seem to see demons under every stone and around every corner! These beliefs can lead to actions as dangerous and violent as those of Legion. As I write there have been disturbing stories in the press about children being ritually murdered because they were believed to be possessed by devils. Even if we reject the idea of demonic possession, the fact remains that some people are severely disturbed mentally, and anguish of spirit is within the experience of us all. During my placement it struck me that the patients were not that different from some of the people I met outside. Many people are overly anxious with unreal fears, others have the strangest ideas, more fantasy than fact, and others have odd, quirky habits, and so on. Push these things a bit further and we would regard these people as mentally ill. Legion stands for the disorder that is present in all of us to some degree, and at the least, we can let his story tell us something about the power of God to bring order to the disturbance of our own lives. Most churches offer the ministry of healing, usually with prayer and the laying on of hands and sometimes anointing. To be prayed over in this way brings inner healing, often in unexpected ways. Seeking healing from God can complement medicinal cures; it can also reach places that conventional medicine cannot. It may be better to let God re-order our lives than to suppress the disorder by drugs.

What are the parts of your life that feel disordered – from compulsive behaviour and irrational fears and anxieties to being pulled this way and that by competing loyalties or the pressures of life? Offer them to Jesus and ask him to speak his words of healing: 'Hush, be still.'

3. Restoring Life
Read Mark 5:21-6:6a
'As soon as Jesus had returned by boat to the other shore, a large crowd gathered around him.' Wherever Jesus went he attracted large numbers of people, and the fact that he did this was a cause of concern to the authorities. Crowds can be unpredictable; they are easily led; feelings are quickly magnified and take over. In a crowd people surrender something of their judgement and individuality – it seems to be overborne by the power of the collective spirit. Jesus never worked the crowds, instead

he taught them and he healed them, and today we reflect on two miracles that brought new life: to a woman in mid-life and to a young girl. In both cases the pressure of the crowd, both physically and mentally, is resisted. It took courage and determination for both Jairus and the woman to get near to Jesus.

The crowd hear Jairus tell Jesus about his daughter and they go with Jesus to Jairus' house. There would have been a sense of awe and anticipation; few would have doubted that Jesus could cure the young girl, but what did they make of him beyond being a wonder-worker? Mark will tell us soon, but as Jesus makes his way he senses that someone had touched his cloak. Mark records that he knew 'at once that power had gone out of him,' and equally instantaneously the woman 'knew within herself that she was cured of her affliction'. When she realises that Jesus is aware that someone had touched him she comes forward; trembling she falls at his feet and tells her story. Not only had she been physically cured, but she had received enough courage to be open about her affliction. It is a wonderful story of faith, and it is this that Jesus commends as he says to her, 'Daughter, your faith has healed you. Go in peace, free from your affliction.'

I imagine it was easier for Jairus to approach Jesus. He was well known, people would have made way for him, and he was accustomed to speaking in public; but even so, to cry for help is not always easy for public figures. For the woman it was harder and (I imagine) more embarrassing – even if people in those days were not so reticent about personal matters as the English! But both tell us something important about persistence and desire as part of faith. In his parable about the unjust judge (Luke 18:1-5) Jesus commends persistence to those who seek God. God longs to makes us whole, to give us his gifts, but we have got to want those gifts; we must desire them with our whole heart, and then 'full measure, pressed down and shaken together and running over will be poured into our laps.' (Luke 6:38) Jesus shows that God responds to persistence and desire. It was so strong in the woman that she is healed as soon as she reaches out to Jesus.

Jairus called out to him in his grief and straightway Jesus went
to his house. Putting aside the ritual mourners, and accompanied
only by the inner three disciples, he takes the girl by the hand
and says the word of life: 'Talitha cum', 'Get up, my child.' The
intimacy of the encounter and the affectionate simplicity of the
cure are a lovely picture of the way God longs to be close to us.
Both healings point beyond the physical cure. The woman is not
just healed, she is made whole, given back her true life as a
woman; and God's gift of new life is shown to have no bounds
when the young girl is brought back from the dead. Mark tells
us that there are no limits to God's power, not even death. The
reach of God is beyond this life. It is the same point that Mark
has made with the stories about the stilling of the storm and the
healing of Legion: God's power goes beyond what we can imagine. These miracles also confirm Mark's deeper point that in
Jesus we see the power of God at work: he is the Son of God.

Some of the people understand this and put their faith in
him, but others, among them those in his home town, do not.
Their response is much the same as that of Jesus' family who
thought that he was out of his mind. Sometimes those who
know us well see beyond the surface of our lives to the potential,
the reality underneath; but not always. Those closest to us can be
set in their opinions; after all they have known us longer than
anyone else, and whatever others may say, they know what we
are like! And this is doubly the case with those who know us a
little, more through reputation than personal encounter. It can
be hard to see the familiar in a new light; we resist it because it
may require us to re-evaluate more than our opinion of the person: our whole outlook may be challenged. This seems to have
been the problem in Nazareth; as they said, 'We know who he is;
he's the carpenter's son, and his sisters and brothers are here
with us. Son of God indeed!' (cf 6:2-3) This is an attitude often
found with religious people, another example of familiarity
clouding our vision. As you reflect today, imagine yourself in
the position of the woman reaching out to touch Jesus. What do
you really want him to do for you? How deeply do you desire
his gifts?

4. Execution

Read Mark 6:6b-29

This section begins with Jesus sending out the twelve – even novices can do the work of God! They must share immediately what they have received. Jesus tells them to take nothing for the journey: those who proclaim the gospel are to be entirely dependent on those whom they serve, and their message will be confirmed by the same deeds of power that Jesus himself has performed. Not only are they to proclaim the good news, they are to warn those who do not listen. Refusing to listen, like any turning away from God, is a sin, and as they leave they must shake off the dust of the town from their feet. This is a powerful gesture, a dramatic way of saying on your heads be it. When pious Jews returned from Gentile lands they shook off the dust from their feet so that nothing from profane places should contaminate the holy land. They dissociated themselves completely from it. By this gesture the disciples say, 'We have shared with you the words of life; if you reject them, then you must bear the consequences.' The aim is repentance rather than condemnation, but Mark reminds us that meeting with Jesus, even if simply through those who speak in his name, is an occasion of judgement – a theme that runs throughout his gospel. After this opening, Mark moves quickly to the story of the execution of John the Baptist.

Jesus' fame had spread and had reached the court of Herod. The people were asking who he was, and Mark sets the story of John's death in the context of the answers they gave. Some thought he was John the Baptist, others Elijah, or one of the prophets. Herod, fearing that his evil deeds were returning to haunt him, believed that Jesus was John brought back to life. Clearly there was something about John that held Herod in thrall; Mark says that he went in awe of John 'knowing him to be a good and holy man'. He liked to hear him, and his words found their mark for 'what he heard left him greatly disturbed.' Herod listened, but he turned away. And when manoeuvred into ordering John's execution he was not strong enough to say 'No.' Herod was more concerned for his reputation in the eyes of his guests and of his new wife and daughter than for his own conscience, and though 'greatly distressed', he ordered John to be beheaded. Not surprisingly, it seemed to him that in Jesus John had returned from the grave with supernatural powers to torment his guilty conscience.

As so often, evil found its opportunity through moral weakness. Herod had repudiated his first wife in favour of Herodias, the wife of his brother Philip, and John the Baptist had been outspoken in his condemnation, voicing the popular opinion that Herod had acted wrongly. Herodias nursed revenge and when the moment came she seized her opportunity. Herod probably thought of himself as a strong ruler; he was certainly powerful enough to be able to get his way, but inwardly he was a weak man. A strong ruler is wise before he is powerful, and Herod was foolish. To stand up for right in the face of Herodias and his guests was more than he could do. Today we would say Herod was concerned for his image. Presenting the right image is a preoccupation of public figures, and often requires an economy with the truth, especially in matters of personal conduct. The connection between private morality and public conduct is a constant theme in human history, and we often hear the argument that what we do in private has no bearing on fitness for public office. I have never been convinced by this argument. Morality is one; pursuing different standards in public and private life is to divide morality and invite failure. It is a sign of inner weakness and lack of wisdom. As Jesus said, a house divided cannot stand (3:25); it is inherently weak. But this is not what the world wants to hear and those, like John the Baptist, who speak up for moral truth in a morally lax age are generally ignored or dismissed as hopelessly outmoded, their views held up to parody and ridicule. But even so, that the house is divided is plain for all to see. On the one hand we live in a militant, secular climate where the press refuses to take the church seriously, and the part that Christianity has played in shaping western values is simply ignored, often wilfully, as with the refusal to acknowledge the Christian heritage of Europe in the Constitution of the European Union. On the other hand there remains a fascination with religion, born perhaps of the widespread sense of a lack of meaning and purpose in life. Like Herod, we are attracted by evident holiness, as the death of Pope John Paul II showed. To move from fascination to commitment, from apathy to fulfilment, requires inner strength, and that comes from being able to name Jesus as Lord.

It is easy to adopt a moralistic stance and to ignore both the compromises that public life requires if anything is to be accomplished, and the extent to which we all live by double standards simply because of the social pressure to conform. The division is within all of us. As you reflect today ask God to show you where your moral commitment needs to be strengthened, and also hold before him those who lead us that they may be led in the path of wisdom.

5. Feeding the Hungry
Read Mark 6:30-end

After recounting briefly the return of the twelve, Mark moves to the story of the feeding of the five thousand. It is one of the stories that features in all four gospels, and the fact that all four evangelists chose to record it shows that it is of considerable significance. Mark alone tells it twice (thus underlining its importance) and its meaning will be considered in the next chapter when we read about the feeding of the four thousand. Mark follows it with the story of Jesus walking on the water and he explicitly links the two episodes.

Whether it was five or four thousand people that were fed from just a few loaves and fishes, the miracle is an astonishing event. So much so that various attempts have been made to rationalise it. It has been suggested that the willingness of a few to give away their food prompted others to match their generosity and share the food that they had in fact brought with them but had kept concealed. Others have suggested that the numbers involved were exaggerated, or that each only received a token amount of food, or that the story is not meant to be taken literally, but is a symbolic picture of how Christ feeds his people. This story and the following one about Jesus walking on the water are of a piece with the others in this section. How do we understand events outside our experience like storms being calmed, madmen being cured, pigs rushing into a lake, people being raised from the dead, and thousands being fed from a few loaves and fishes? The temptation, as with the feeding of the five thousand, is to rationalise the stories, or to treat them as purely symbolic stories. The problem is that there is no evidence that Mark (and the other evangelists) saw them as purely symbolic stories, and if they were, why would they have bothered to record them? Miracles were not a new phenomenon – there are stories about rabbis altering the weather as well as curing the sick – and miracle cures are known in our own day. Mark and the other evangelists record them to open our eyes to the truth about Jesus, and there would have been little point in doing so if the events recorded had not taken place. It is significant that the original Greek of the New Testament does not use the equivalent word for 'miracle' – which means merely a marvellous thing, something to be wondered at – instead they are described as 'acts of power' or a 'sign'. What we call a miracle is a sign pointing to a truth beyond the actual event. The point is put well by C. F. D. Moule in his commentary on St Mark's gospel:

It seems that, wherever Jesus went, surprising things did happen. But the importance of them lay not in their marvellous quality: they were not, like conjuring tricks, merely astonishing; nor were they ever done merely in order to surprise. They always seem to have been the result, simply, of his concern for people and his perfect and absolute obedience, as Son of God, to the will of his Father. We assume quite correctly, that there is a regularity and consistency about nature, and that effect can always be relied upon to follow cause …. What we forget is that we have never ourselves witnessed a situation in which persons needing help are reached by a man perfectly in line with God's will …. Might it not be that what we call a miracle would be the natural and inevitable effect, given such a cause, and given also enough faith – trust in God – on the part of the other persons concerned? That is why these miracles are called acts of power: they are natural phenomena, whenever the power of God is let through by obedience and concern for persons and by a readiness to trust God.

(C. F. D. Moule, *The Gospel According to St Mark*, pp 15-16)

As we have seen (6:5), not even Jesus was able to work miracles in all situations. Where the personal relationship and the response of faith is lacking he cannot impose the will of God. But when these things are present, and men and women put themselves at the disposal of God, then very striking things happen. Where God's sovereignty is really acknowledged lives are made whole and evil is overcome. When Jesus walked over the lake to the disciples, Mark says they were terrified, thinking it was a ghost, and he comments on their response: 'They had not understood the incident of the loaves; their minds were closed.' Mark says, in effect, that the disciples had not seen beyond the wonder of the miracle to the truth to which it pointed.

These stories challenge our modern way of thinking and raise some difficult questions about the way we understand scripture. They also offer a profound assurance about the power of God in Christ. These two things pull against one another, for the assurance would not be true if the stories were false or simply symbolic. When faced with a biblical event wholly beyond our experience the path of wisdom is not credulity, nor rejection; rather we should hold it together with our modern scientific knowledge and let the tension between them draw us forward into God's greater truth. As you reflect today try to let this tension draw you forward into a deeper experience of the power of God.

6. True Security

In this section of his gospel Mark shows us powerfully that Jesus is God's new beginning, and in the miracle stories the underlying theme of the first section, the question of authority, again comes to the fore but in a new way. Jesus not only speaks but acts with the authority and the power of God. And because he does so, St Mark says, we can put our trust in him even when we are tossed about on the seas of life. In his meditations on priesthood, *Light in the Lord*, Cardinal Hume wrote, 'I think so much of our ministry is rowing against the wind. That is my experience, the sense of being on my own. It is then that Jesus says, "Take courage".' Many Christians, and not just priests, often feel the same. It is then that we need to turn to God and ask him to renew our trust in him. The story of Israel, of which the coming of Jesus was the fulfilment, is a story of a people who lived by trust in God. The stories that Mark recounts in this section both ask a question and offer an assurance: Where do you place your trust? Trust in God for none can overcome his power, and his love will never fail. Trust is like love – indeed the two terms are, to an extent, interchangeable. Like love, trust is one of the basic ingredients of being human. It is not possible to live a meaningful human life unless we learn to trust another. The relationships that sustain us are relationships of trust; take trust away and we atrophy as people. So Mark's question is one of the basic questions of life, Where do we place our trust? Or, to put it another way, Where do we look for security?

It is an important question because in today's world security is in short supply. Its not just the threat from terrorism, but the things that gave us a sense of security seem themselves under siege – the family, marriage, employment, the welfare state, common values – so much so that it is difficult to describe our world as trusting. In this climate of fear and insecurity many are tempted to put their trust in the various groups and sects today offering a way to inner peace, physical healing, union with God. Some attract considerable followings even when their claims and their way of life seem crazy and destructive, like the sect at Waco in Texas that, some years ago, ended in a shoot-out with the police. These groups are not really concerned with setting people free, but with keeping them in bondage, often to the leader. In their hands people are diminished; God is excluded and so there is no growth.

Another temptation is to put our trust in material things, or in politics. The last century was marked by false hopes on a grand scale. Fascism, communism, liberalism, science and the free market have all been looked to as harbingers of the new age. They have all been found wanting. The result has been death not life; a death of the spirit, an inner decay. We see the signs of this in various ways: in the pursuit of escapism through drug and alcohol abuse, sex and deviant pleasures; we see it in the rising levels of violence, particularly against children, and of anti-social behaviour; we see it also in the rise of religious fundamentalism. We have all to some extent been seduced by false hopes, putting our trust in the gods of the age and their false promises, like the incessant and insidious temptation that the way to happiness is to take out a loan, that is to get further into debt (and thus into bondage) – described seductively by the banks as extending our credit.

Rowing against the wind is hard work and what keeps me going is the conviction that God offers a better hope than the gods of the age. The gospels do not answer all our questions, and pose some difficult challenges to our modern understanding, but they show us enough to know that God is not only to be trusted, he is the source of trust. It is in our relationship with him that we shall find our true security. In Jesus we see the life that trust in God makes possible. Perhaps the time has come to ask ourselves the question: Where do I look for security and place my trust? Am I following a way of life that sets me free or that keeps me bound and prevents me from growing?

III

True Righteousness
Chapters 7 & 8:1-26

Introduction

In the New English Bible chapter seven of Mark's gospel is headed 'Growing Tension'. As the story unfolds, the running dispute between Jesus and the Pharisees worsens. Jesus clearly posed a major threat because he struck at the foundations of their way of life; and indeed at the whole basis of Israelite religion. So they sought him out and challenged him. Jesus' response was robust, if not insulting: he accused them of hypocrisy. Eight centuries before, Isaiah had accused Israel of the same fault: 'this people worship me with empty words and pay me lip service while their hearts are far from me, and their religion is but a human precept, learnt by rote.' So, said Isaiah, God would visit them and 'the wisdom of their wise men will vanish and the discernment of the discerning will be lost.' (Isaiah 29:13, 14) The Pharisees were no match for Jesus, and later in the gospel Mark tells us that he silenced all those who tried to catch him out. (12:34) Jesus had indeed set their wisdom at naught and confounded their discernment.

At the heart of the dispute was the basic question of personal righteousness; as St Paul was later to put it: Is it by works or grace that we are justified? The Pharisees were the 'separated brethren', they kept themselves apart in order that they might worship God in a state of ritual purity and strictly in accordance with the law. To be told that they, of all people, were the ones of whom Isaiah spoke was too much to bear. No doubt many of the Pharisees were good and holy people, but the attention they gave to the minutiae of the law meant that they could not see the wood for the trees. St Matthew gives a longer account of Jesus' dispute with them in which he records Jesus' most stinging re-

buke: 'Alas for you, scribes and Pharisees, hypocrites! You pay
tithes of mint and dill and cummin; but you have overlooked the
weightier demands of the law – justice, mercy, and good faith. It
is these you should have practised, without neglecting the
others. Blind guides! You strain off a midge, yet gulp down a
camel!' (Matthew 23:23-24) Centuries before, Micah had put it
beautifully when he said, 'The Lord has told you what is good,
and what it is that the Lord requires of you: only to act justly, to
love loyalty, and to walk humbly with your God.' (Micah 6:8)
And Amos, in a passage sharply critical of ritual worship, says,
'Instead let justice flow on like a river and righteousness like an
everlasting stream.' (Amos 5:24) The prophets had foreseen a
time when God would write his law upon their hearts (e.g.
Ezekiel 36:25-28). Jesus was the fulfilment of that prophecy; he
taught that purity of heart came first; that, rather than the zeal-
ous keeping of the law, made a person acceptable to God. It was
radical stuff, literally going to the root of what religion was all
about.

The danger of Pharisaism is twofold: on the one hand it can
reduce religion to outward observance, and on the other it can
produce a spiritual elite. Israel compounded this second danger
with its racial and religious exclusivity. Despite their attacks, the
Pharisees must have been impressed by Jesus; after all there was
no doubting the cures that he performed, and the people hung
on his words and marvelled at his deeds: 'All that he does, he
does well; he even makes the deaf hear and the dumb speak.'
(7:37) Confounded, they ask for a sign, something that would
put his authority beyond doubt. Alas those who are trapped in
their ways can neither see nor hear, nor can they confess that
Jesus fulfils the scriptures that they know so well. The section
ends with Jesus warning the disciples against the leaven of the
Pharisees. They do not understand him, neither does he spell
out his meaning, even though he shows them how they might
put two-and-two together. The disciples, like the Pharisees, have
to see with their inner eyes; true holiness comes from within;
they must work out the truth for themselves. Jesus will not give

them a sign beyond the works that he does and the words that he speaks.

1. Defiled Hands

Read Mark 7:1-13

Almost as soon as Jesus began his ministry the Pharisees began to seek ways in which they could bring about Jesus' death. (3.6) This atmosphere of hostility meant that Jesus was constantly watched, the risk being that any slip, however trivial, could be used to found an accusation against him. We see this constant harassment in the police states of our own times. Watching Jesus and his companions, the Pharisees noticed that some of the disciples failed to wash their hands before eating. Mark feels that his readers might wonder at the religious significance of this, and so he adds a note explaining that the Pharisees and the Jews in general never eat without washing the hands, in obedience to an old-established tradition. (It is from asides like this that scholars infer that Mark must have been writing for non-Jewish readers.) So the Pharisees came to Jesus and asked: 'Why do your disciples not conform to the ancient tradition, but eat food with defiled hands?' Jesus is not intimidated and replies in forthright terms: 'Isaiah was right when he prophesied about you hypocrites in these words: "These people pay me lip service, but their heart is far from me: their worship of me is in vain, for they teach as doctrines the commandment of men." You neglect the commandment of God, in order to maintain the tradition of men.' (cf Isaiah 29:13)

As we have seen, at the root of the dispute between Jesus and the Pharisees was the question: What makes a man righteous, or acceptable to God? Central to the Jewish religion is Torah, the Law, the rules and commands set out in the first five books of the Bible. Their purpose was to regulate the nation so that it operated on principles which were God-given; in this way Israel would be a righteous nation and its people acceptable to God. There can be no doubt that these laws represented a huge advance on the moral codes of the times, and in many respects still form the foundation of civilised society. Law does have an important part to play in religious life, but the Pharisees had taken it to extremes. The six hundred and more commandments had been expanded over the centuries into a detailed code, the aim of which was to provide guidance on every aspect of life. Where God was concerned nothing was to be left to chance. The Law prohibited working on the Sabbath, so it was important to define what constituted 'work'; the law restricted travel on the Sabbath, so a 'Sabbath day's journey' had to be defined. And so it went on, and included washing the hands before meals.

The Pharisees were the strictest group in Israel and prided themselves on their meticulous keeping of the law. This was, quite simply, impossible for most people. The righteousness of the Pharisees was the righteousness of an elite. Jesus taught that God's concern was with the ordinary people, on whom the spiritual elite looked down. He sat light to their laws. Righteousness, he said, was basically about inner intentions, not outward deeds. His disciples might not have washed their hands before eating; that might mean they became ill, but it did not mean that they were unacceptable before God. He was hot in his condemnation of those who argued otherwise. It was not the law of God that they were defending, but their own tradition. Worse still, in many cases they had devised traditions that were contrary to the law of God. No wonder he called them hypocrites!

It is, of course, easy to see the faults of others and not of oneself. Many have applied Jesus' accusations against the Pharisees to the church, and with justification. Christians are not free from pettifogging concerns and the maintenance of the minutiae of tradition, and it always gets in the way of the gospel. Today as you reflect ask God to help you focus on the big picture and to see clearly what in the tradition is essential and what is not.

2. Pure Hearts
Read Mark 7:14-23
To many in Israel the food laws must have been a major problem. Among other things they were divisive because not every-

one could keep them. Animals were divided into two categories, clean and unclean. Contact with unclean food brought ritual defilement, and anyone contaminated in this way was excluded from the worshipping community. Removing the taint of defilement involved much ritual washing, which was very time-consuming, and literally impossible for shepherds and others who had to earn their living in harsh, outdoor conditions. Many of the people must have spent their lives in a ritually unclean state. They had given up on religion. Mark tells us that Jesus repudiated these laws: 'On another occasion he called the people and said to them, "Listen to me, all of you, and understand this: nothing that goes into a person from outside can defile him; no, it is the things that come out of a person that defile him".' It was such a radical departure from tradition that the disciples failed to grasp the full meaning of what Jesus had said, and they asked him about it when they were alone with him. He explained it again, and then, in case anyone has still missed the point St Mark spells it out: 'By saying this he declared all foods clean.' It doesn't matter what you eat, defilement comes from the wrong inner attitude; eating will defile you if it amounts to gluttony, for that is your inner attitude to the food, but the food itself is neutral.

Jesus gives other examples of the things that defile us: 'evil thoughts, acts of fornication, theft, murder, adultery, greed, and malice; fraud, indecency, envy, slander, arrogance and folly'. These things, he says, come from the human heart. One of the things that distinguished the religion of Moses from that of the surrounding nations was its moral code. Today we take for granted that killing, theft, adultery and the other prohibitions in the Ten Commandments are wrong, but when they were first promulgated they were startling and revolutionary, some of them marking a sharp break from the customs and and practices of the peoples of the ancient Near East among whom the Israelites dwelt. 'They represented a giant leap forward in the conception of man's relationship to man and to God.' (Moshe Pearlman, *In the Footsteps of Moses*, p 114) In the thirteenth century BC sacred prostitution and orgiastic fertility rites were the norm,

and rulers treated their peoples harshly; religion was about pro-
pitiating the gods; morality was no part of worship. Moses believed otherwise, as did the prophets after him. Jesus is the heir
to this prophetic tradition. He affirms the prophets' teaching
about the connection between morality and righteousness, and
he places it above the traditions of the Pharisees and the accepted
notions of what made people acceptable to God.

It was not simply personal immorality that the prophets denounced. Amos, for example, thundered at those who oppressed
the helpless and ground down the poor, perverted justice, imposed unjust taxes, and lounged in luxury and indolence. (Amos
4:1; 5:7, 10; 6:1-7) Malachi says God will judge those 'who cheat
the hired labourer of his wages, who wrong the widow and the
fatherless, [and] who thrust the alien aside.' (Malachi 3:5) The
prophets also condemned the use of false weights and measures
in the market (Amos 8:5, 6). In the 'Law of Holiness' (Leviticus
chs 17-27) rules about Temple ritual are placed together with
rules about agriculture, trading in the market, criminal offences
and personal morality. No distinction is made between them;
they are all equally part of worship. Just as the Pharisees lost
sight of the weightier demands of justice and good faith, so
today we have lost sight of the truth that what we do in the market place is as much a part of our worship as what we do in the
holy place. Morality is one; it unites the personal with the political and the economic. This for some will be no less a revolution
in outlook than were the laws of Moses in his day.

Pure hearts require true morals. Jesus may have abrogated
the food laws, and rescued the people from a tangle of pettifogging rules, but his way is no less demanding. However, he is not
moralistic; that would simply substitute moral purity for ritual
purity as the test of righteousness. Jesus knows that we shall sin;
it is a fact of life. We are not condemned because we sin, but only
if we fail to acknowledge our sin and turn away from it. To those
who genuinely do so he reaches out in forgiveness and restores
them to his fellowship. This does not take the seriousness out of
the moral struggle, but it does remove the self-concern.

Reflect today on what your behaviour, at home and at work, says about your inner attitudes. The seven deadly sins are pride, anger, lust, gluttony, envy, avarice and sloth: Where do you feel you let yourself down? Ask God to give you a pure heart.

3. Scraps for the Dogs
Read Mark 7:24-end

After this confrontation with the Pharisees Jesus moves to the far north, to Gentile lands, and here two more people are cured, a young girl and a man who was both deaf and dumb. Mark tells us that Jesus wanted to remain alone, but that was impossible, and as soon as he had arrived he was sought out by a Phoenician woman from Syria whose daughter was unwell. She begged Jesus to heal her daughter, but in terms surprising to our ears he, at first, refuses. On this occasion it is the dialogue rather than the cure that is important for Mark. The woman does not take offence at being described as a 'dog' – to this day a supreme insult in the Middle East – instead she turns the remark around and says that even the dogs can feed from the scraps that fall from the master's table. It would be nice to know the temper of the exchange and the facial expressions and gestures of Jesus and the woman: what was said unspoken might have imparted a very different character to the exchange. As it stands the dialogue suggests that Jesus believed that his mission was to the Jews and not the Gentiles, and that the woman accepted this. Even so, she persisted, believing that Jesus would not refuse to help her. And she was right; no firm line can be drawn in the face of suffering, and he assures her that her daughter is well.

Who is in and who is out is a question that bedevils religion. We see it in the church with the disputes about who shall be saved, who may be admitted to holy communion, baptised, married, and so on. Division and separation is part of the story of Israel. When the Israelites entered Canaan it was, they believed, through an act of God who drove out the nations before them and gave them their land. Thereafter a policy of racial separateness was pursued. When, after the Babylonian Exile, the

Jews were restored to the land under Ezra and Nehemiah this policy was enforced and the Israelites commanded to put away their foreign wives. (See Ezra chs 9 and 10, and also Nehemiah 10:30; 13:3, 23-28) These episodes, and the Exodus, and the conquest of Canaan, raise some very difficult questions about the character of God. Can we really believe that the God of love revealed by Jesus simultaneously punished Pharaoh and hardened his heart so that he did not learn from the punishment, thus justifying harsher action and more terrible plagues? It came as a relief to me when I realised that the Old Testament contains a number of pictures of God which show that understanding developed and changed over the centuries. The high point was reached in the sixth century BC. In the middle part of Isaiah we see a conception of God much closer to the Christian understanding of God as the God of all nations who saves his people by taking their sinfulness upon himself, and not by leading them to victory in battle. (Isaiah 52:13-53-end) However, it has to be said that Jesus seems to have accepted 'a fairly sharp distinction between Jew and Gentile as part of God's plan, and regarded his commission, and that of his disciples, as being limited to Israel.' (D. E. Nineham, *Saint Mark*, p 199.) Even so, he seems not to have taken a narrow view of this limited mission, and faced with real need he was prepared to make an exception. Indeed in the parable of the Good Samaritan, told by Luke, he taught that the fact of human need took precedence over the restrictions imposed by race and ritual purity. The early church developed this thinking and saw that God's salvation in Christ was not just for the Jews but for all people. This was the clear meaning of Peter's vision at Joppa of the sail-cloth full of creatures (Acts 10), and St Paul developed this into a theology of reconciliation. Writing to the Ephesians he said, 'Once you were far off, but now in union with Christ Jesus you have been brought near through the shedding of Christ's blood. For he is himself our peace. Gentiles and Jews, he has made the two one, and in his own body of flesh and blood has broken down the barrier of enmity which separated them.' (Ephesians 2:13, 14) The New People of God, as the first

Christians saw themselves, established a community across the natural boundaries of race, nation and clan, 'and it was precisely this transracial and transnational character of the people that was so deeply impressive in the early centuries and that seemed like the advent of a new humanity.' (John Macquarrie, *The Faith of the People of God*, p 10)

St Mark follows the story of the Syro-Phoenician woman with the healing of the deaf mute. This, and the two miracles that follow (the feeding of the Four Thousand and the cure of the blind man) make more explicit Jesus' identity as the Messiah. The healing miracles are an enactment of the messianic signs prophesied by Isaiah: '"Be strong, fear not! Your God comes to save you ..." Then the eyes of the blind will be opened, and the ears of the deaf unstopped. The lame will leap like a deer, and the dumb will shout aloud ...' (Isaiah 35:4-6) For those with eyes to see and ears to hear it is clear who Jesus is. Despite his instructions, the news is spread abroad, and a confrontation with the religious authorities made all the more certain. What is at stake is not just the customs and traditions of the Pharisees, but their whole understanding of who God is and for whom he is God.

As you reflect today think about the character of God: if we believe that Jesus is the Messiah, the Son of God, then he must reveal truly what God is like – as Bishop Michael Ramsay put it, there is nothing in God that is un-Christlike. And previous revelations, including much in the Old Testament, must be re-read in that light.

4. The Sign of the Loaves
Read Mark 8:1-10
Between the cures of the deaf mute and the blind man Mark places an account of another feeding miracle, this time of four thousand people. Like the previous feeding of the five thousand, it is a messianic sign. Christians today with their experience of the Eucharist naturally understand it as a foretaste of the Lord's Supper. Indeed, in the early church the parallels would have been clearer because at the distribution of Holy Communion

they remained seated, like the crowd, and the deacons brought round to them the loaves blessed and broken by the celebrant. But this was not evident to those who were there at the time who lacked our experience, and it is not entirely surprising that the disciples did not immediately understand the significance of what Jesus did.

Mark tells us that both miracles were performed in 'remote' places, and that despite the large number of people and the meagre offering of food, everyone ate their fill. The parallel is with the journey of the Israelites in the wilderness when God provided abundant food for his people. The miracles also recall the occasion when Elisha fed one hundred men with twenty barley loaves and some fresh, ripe grain; despite his servant's protest that the food was insufficient, 'they ate and had some left over.' (2 Kings 4:42-44) For those with eyes to see, as he feeds the people, Jesus fulfils the law and the prophets, as the Messiah was expected to do. Moreover, the banquet was an image of heaven, a foretaste of the blessed destiny of the faithful: 'On this mountain the Lord of hosts will prepare a banquet of rich fare for all the peoples, a banquet of wines well matured, richest fare and well-matured wines strained clear.' (Isaiah 25:6; see also Isaiah 55:1-3) In Psalm 132 the Lord swears to David that if his successors are faithful Israel will be his resting place, and he 'will bless her with food in plenty and satisfy her needy with bread.' (Psalm 132:14, 15) Jesus would have been very aware of these images in the religious heritage of Israel, and in providing abundant food for his followers he was anticipating the Messianic Banquet, and indicating that he, as host, was the One who was to come, the Messiah.

One of the images we use to interpret the Eucharist is the foretaste of the heavenly banquet. In our communion with God and with each other we anticipate heaven, the fulfilment of God's promise that he will dwell among his people. (Revelation 21:3) A shared meal is a sign of unity and peace, as Victor de Waal explains: 'The eating of a common meal, the sharing of the same food which is absorbed as the very substance of our body has always been recognised, and is so still, as the effective symbol of the unity of a family, and of peace between men who have been strangers or at variance with one another.' (Victor de Waal, *What is the Church?*, p 50) Jesus used table fellowship as a sign that those commonly held to be beyond the pale, sinners and bad characters, were not rejected by God. The Pharisees criticised him, and asked the disciples, 'Why does he eat with tax collectors and sinners?' He overheard the question and responded that it was not the healthy that needed a doctor, but the sick: 'I did not come to call the virtuous, but sinners.' (Mark 2:15-17) The Eucharistic fellowship is not made up of the virtuous alone; all are welcome so long as we are prepared to repent of our sins and desire to lead a new life. And as the bread and wine are shared it is a foretaste of that new life that we receive.

When it was first celebrated the Eucharist was a proper meal; this is still its basis, but in its present form much of the symbolism of the shared meal has been lost. St Paul urges the unity symbolised by the Eucharist upon the Corinthian church in which division was rife: 'Because there is one loaf, we, though many, are one body; for it is one loaf of which we all partake.' (1 Corinthians 10:17) Sharing bread with another and drinking from the same cup are also deeply symbolic acts. I have a poster with a text by Mark Link that reads: 'To share a cup is to share each other's fate. To share a loaf is to share each other's blessing.' Victor de Waal develops this symbolism: 'The cup that is shared symbolises the Christian's participation in the new covenant; the bread broken and distributed, his membership of the one body, the body which Jesus had declared to be his own.' (*What is the Church?*, pp 49-50) Joining Jesus in his mission – sharing his fate – we also receive his blessing. As with the feeding of the crowds, when we offer what have to God our resources are extended and become adequate for our work. God takes what we offer and uses it to build the kingdom.

Think today about your experience of the Eucharist, and the parallels with Jesus feeding the multitudes, and his table fellowship with sinners and bad characters. Reflect, too, about the communal character of the celebration. As you worship, ask God to deepen within you the experience of unity with him and with your fellow worshippers.

5. Give us a Sign
Read Mark 8:11-26

With an ironic touch, Mark introduces at this point the account of the Pharisees asking Jesus for a sign. In the light of what has just been described, a series of miracles of astonishing power and deep symbolic meaning, it is an extraordinary and insulting request. No wonder Jesus sighed deeply – his sigh must have spoken volumes – and refused their request. You can hear his exasperation: 'Why does this generation ask for a sign? Truly I tell you: no sign shall be given to this generation.' It is important to note that the Pharisees asked for 'a sign from heaven'. When the people saw what Jesus did they said that a great prophet had risen among them; and even though Jesus performed the Messianic signs, the penny still did not drop. In the eyes of the Pharisees even extraordinary miracles like the feeding of thousands and the stilling of storms, were not sufficient to establish Jesus' claim to be the Messiah. They wanted something that put the matter utterly beyond doubt, an apocalyptic portent whose meaning was unambiguous. From the Pharisees' point of view this was, perhaps, not unreasonable; after all, Jesus sat light to the Law and permitted people to break its provisions. One of the pillars of the faith that went back to Moses was at stake, and if it was to be changed, then the authority of him who made the changes must be unchallengeable: only a sign from heaven could put the matter beyond dispute.

I wonder if the heavens had opened, as Mark tells us they did at Jesus' baptism, the Pharisees would have been convinced. There are other occasions in the gospels when the heavens opened but not everyone understood what had happened (see e.g. John 12:29). Signs are ambivalent; their interpretation depends on the perspective of the observer, and it seems to me, they never come with a visible guarantee, *Made in Heaven*. We see this in our own attempts to read the signs of the times. If ever there was a sign from heaven about the wrongness of our ways, global warming is it. But as I write the US administration refuses to accept the evidence, and among those who do there are different views about how to read it. Does it present us with a technological problem – how to develop cleaner energy so that we can continue with present levels of consumption; or does it present us with a moral problem – how to reduce consumption so that our demand for energy will be reduced and the earth's resources better conserved?

Not all the Pharisees were opposed to Jesus; some of them became his followers, and, we may assume, others were attracted but remained uncommitted. Many people today feel like that about religion. Many more people than those who go to church say they believe in God, and Jesus remains an attractive figure, but commitment is another thing. 'If only there was a clear sign; something that put the matter beyond doubt; then we would believe.' I doubt it. Asking for a sign is often a way of avoiding commitment; it helps us to remain on the fence because in our heart we know that signs are not, in themselves, convincing. Faith is a matter of looking at the evidence and being prepared to move where it points even though it falls short of clear proof. Faith is both a choice to believe and something given. We have seen that Jesus taught in parables to awaken faith, and in the same way his miracles point beyond the miraculous to a deeper meaning, but we have to work it out for ourselves. Mark ends this section with a story that makes the point. As they row across the lake, the disciples misunderstand Jesus' words about the leaven of the Pharisees; they think he is talking about bread – which they have forgotten to bring with them. In the same way they had misunderstood the miracles; they had seen the signs but not where they pointed. Jesus does not spell out their meaning; instead he tells them to use their eyes and ears, and points them in the right direction by referring to the number of baskets of scraps left over. They must work it out for themselves. To be told is not to know; knowledge comes from within, just like the things that defile us. The section ends with a blind man receiving his sight, in two stages. True sight is what the disciples must seek. They have experienced the first stage: they have seen Jesus as a worker of miracles; they must go to the second stage and see him also as the Son of God.

In Jesus God has given us all the signs that we need, though perhaps not all that we want. Picture yourself in the boat with Jesus and the disciples: How would you have seen him at that moment? How do you see him now?

6. Law or Grace?

One of the big questions is: What do we have to do to be accepted by God? The secular character of our age does not mean that it has not gone away, merely that we formulate it in different terms. People still need to feel that they are accepted, that they are loved even when their lives are in a mess; and most people, I think, feel that they are accountable for what they do, even if they cannot name to whom. In this section Mark gives the answer: to be accepted by God we need to have faith in him, and that is an inner disposition rather than outward behaviour. This answer is presented in the context of Jesus' continuing dispute with the Pharisees. There were many examples of personal holiness among the Pharisees, and it would be wrong to suggest that they were unaware of the importance of the inner journey, but nevertheless they were the ones who set themselves the task of keeping the Law in all its particulars, and it is that which marked them out. It was on this aspect of their spirituality that Jesus challenged them, and Mark records another graphic example of the authority that Jesus claimed, an authority that permitted him to set aside part of the Torah, the Law of God.

It took time for Jesus' followers to accept such a radical break with tradition. When Peter in a dream saw a sail cloth full of unclean creatures, he was shocked at the command to kill and eat, protesting that no unclean thing had ever passed his lips (Acts 10). And while the church has not followed Israel in laying down detailed codes of behaviour, we are nevertheless guilty of turning religion into a set of rules, and being too concerned with external matters. Perhaps the real failure of the Pharisees was to look for security in a code. Jesus taught that security could only be found in a relationship, first with God and then with the community. Relationships are things of the Spirit, and the Christian version of Pharisaism often comes from failing to follow where the Spirit leads. Some Christians turn the Bible into a rule book, failing to appreciate its different moods and styles; others see the church as a club, concerned with who is in and who is out, ignoring its mission to be a light to the world. On the charismatic side, fine distinctions are made about the proper manifestation of the gifts of the Spirit, and standing in the church is determined accordingly; while on the Catholic side, a legalistic conception of both the church and its ministers makes the Eucharist, the sacrament of unity, a cause of division. Many Christians take their lead from the secular world, and make a wholly unscriptural division between public and private life, with the gospel excluded from public and business affairs. An equally unscriptural moralism defines attitudes towards those divorced who want to re-marry, and a host of other contemporary problems.

In contrast, Mark shows that Jesus taught a way to God that everyone could follow. No one was excluded from approaching God just because they could not keep all the religious rules. The church is a community of forgiven sinners, not a spiritual elite. Being accepted by God is more about the willingness to make a journey than believing a set of propositions or living by a set of rules. As John Macquarrie has said, 'Faith is more inclusive than belief. It is a total attitude toward life, and although belief is part of this attitude, its essence is rather to be seen in commitment to a way of life.' (*The Faith of the People of God*, p 11) The journey begins when we see what Jesus did as signs rather than wonders, and chose to follow where they point even though we are unsure of the way. This way of faith is actually more demanding than the way of the Pharisees because it places the emphasis on our inner state, and not simply on our outward deeds. It requires trust and not just obedience.

It is the pure in heart whom Jesus called blessed. Purity of heart is something we may desire, but we cannot acquire it by our own unaided efforts. We need to see our faith as both a choice and also as a gift. Opening ourselves to receive the gifts that our choice has made available is central to spiritual growth. Purity of heart is one of these gifts, and it comes over time. Prayer is one of the traditional Lenten disciplines, and it is by deepening our prayer life that our hearts are changed. Prayer strengthens our relationship with God, and allows him to touch our hearts. It does not have to be dramatic or arduous, but it does have to be regular and persistent. The Benedictine method described in the Introduction is a tried and tested way, and through it many have found both a deeper and a livelier faith, a change of heart, and acceptance by God. It is not easy in today's busy world to find the time to pray, but the time has come to try, or try again.

Yet even now, says the Lord,
Turn back to me wholeheartedly
With fasting, weeping and mourning.
Rend your hearts and not your garments,
and turn back to the Lord your God ...' (Joel 2:12,13)

IV

Follow Me
Chapters 8:27-10

Introduction

Mark has now reached the turning point of his gospel. Jesus' ministry in Galilee is concluded; the focus shifts to Jerusalem, and the shadow of the cross falls over the story. Jesus begins to teach the disciples 'that the Son of Man had to endure great suffering, and to be rejected by the elders, the chief priests, and scribes; to be put to death, and to rise again three days afterwards. He spoke about it plainly.' He also teaches them that if this is to be his fate, then it will be theirs also; indeed he tells this not just to the disciples but to all his followers: 'Anyone who wants to be a follower of mine must renounce self; he must take up his cross and follow me.'

Mark illustrates what Jesus means in some of the stories that follow. When the disciples argue about who is the greatest, Jesus sets a child in front of them, the least in the family. Rather than be concerned about their own status, they should be concerned about those who are counted least, for in receiving them they are receiving him: and 'whoever receives me, receives not me but the One who sent me.' The rich young man who kept all the law and yet wanted to know what he must do to win eternal life is told to sell all that he has. Riches, says Jesus, are a great barrier to renouncing self; it is easier for a camel to go through the eye of a needle than for a rich man to enter the kingdom of God. (10:25) When James and John boast that they can drink the cup that Jesus drinks and be baptised with the baptism that he is baptised with (a reference to his coming passion), they are told that that indeed will be their fate. (James was in fact the first of the disciples to die for his faith in Jesus: Acts 12:1, 2.)

The disciples are slow to understand what Jesus says, and

they did not do so until after the resurrection. The problem was all bound up with their expectations. For centuries the Jews had looked forward to the coming of the Messiah who, they believed, would be the One who would set Israel free. Luke records this belief in his story of the two companions who were walking to Emmaus after the crucifixion. When Jesus joins them as they walk along, their faces full of sadness, he asks them why they are downcast. Clopas replies that their hopes have been disappointed. They had been hoping that the prophet Jesus of Nazareth, whom the authorities had crucified, 'was to be the liberator of Israel.' (Luke 24:21) 'Great David's greater son', as the hymn puts it, was expected to restore the fortunes of Israel as David himself had done. He would be God's anointed representative who would restore God's people to their true destiny, and bring in the kingdom or sovereignty of God. The Messiah was to be a political figure, a warrior even, and many hoped Jesus would lead them as David had done, and deliver them from their enemies. St John records that after the feeding of the five thousand the people recognised the miracle as a messianic sign, and Jesus, fearing that they would seize him to proclaim him king, escaped from them into the hills. (John 6:14, 15)

The liberation that Jesus promised was not political or military. God was not the tribal champion of Israel; he was God of all peoples, and he would save them by taking upon himself the burden of their sin, bearing the punishment that was theirs, and setting them free to worship him in spirit and in truth. The sovereignty of God would be enthroned in their hearts, not in their land. It is significant that Jesus refers to himself as 'the Son of Man' rather than the Messiah. The meaning of this phrase is much debated. It can simply mean 'a man', but in the Book of Daniel it has a more representative meaning, a human figure standing for those ready to accept death rather than forswear their allegiance to God, and to whom everlasting sovereignty was given. (Daniel 7:9-14) On Jesus' lips 'Son of Man' implied a victory 'for that utter loyalty to God which wins through, not by force of arms, not by killing and conquering, but by its readiness to go, defenceless, even to the length of death. It stands for the sovereignty of absolute devotion to God.' (C. F. D. Moule, *Saint Mark*, p 66) After the resurrection the first Christians turned to the Book of Isaiah for images to explain the kind of Messiah that Jesus was. There they found the so-called 'Servant Songs' which seemed to foretell precisely the figure of Jesus as one sent by God. We hear the fourth Song (Isaiah 52:13-53 end) read on Good Friday, and its words have become familiar as part of Handel's Messiah:

He was despised, shunned by all,
pain-wracked and afflicted by disease;
we despised him, we held him of no account,
an object from which people turn away their eyes.
Yet it was our afflictions he was bearing,
our pain he endured,
while we thought of him as smitten by God,
struck down by disease and misery.
But he was pierced for our transgressions,
crushed for our iniquities;
the chastisement he bore was health for us
and by his wounds we are healed.
We had all strayed like sheep,
each of us going his own way,
but the Lord laid on him
the guilt of us all. (Isaiah 53:3-6)

The Son of Man will indeed liberate his people – from false ideas and false hopes, and from the power of sin. His victory will be over the forces of evil, the great enemy of God, rather than the enemies of Israel.

1. Who Do You Say I Am?
Read Mark 8:27-9:1
This is the big question, and the background to it is all that the disciples have so far experienced: the teaching, the table fellowship, and the miracles. Have the disciples moved beyond seeing Jesus as an authoritative teacher and astounding miracle worker?

He leads up to the question by asking them first about who the people say he is. The response has been foreshadowed in the story of the murder of John the Baptist: 'Some say John the Baptist, others Elijah, others one of the prophets.' These were the figures who were regarded as preparing the way for the Messiah, and it seems the people could not see beyond the preparatory stage and regarded Jesus as another forerunner. The people had seen the signs but not where they pointed. Jesus repeats the question, but this time directed at the disciples themselves, have they seen the deeper truth? 'And you, who do you say I am?' Peter sees where Jesus is leading and replies, 'You are the Messiah.' It is not clear whether he speaks for himself or for all, but what is clear (from the subsequent exchange) is that he has not appreciated the kind of Messiah that Jesus is. Peter rejects as unthinkable the idea that Jesus will suffer and die.

At the end of the last section we saw how Jesus opened the eyes of a blind man in two stages. This, perhaps, is used by Mark to illustrate the two stages of the opening of the disciples' eyes, and indeed the two stages in which all our eyes are opened – that is the two stages beyond wonder and amazement at Jesus' teaching and miracles. Peter's reply that Jesus is the Messiah is the first stage. He follows the logic of the second question, with its repeated stress on 'you', and realises that Jesus is expecting a different answer to that of the people. Perhaps Peter has seen where the signs point; perhaps, still following Jesus' lead, he grasps what the expected answer must be; either way the realisation dawns, and he makes his confession. The second stage is to grasp the full implications of the answer, namely that Jesus is the Messiah in the sense that he will die a redemptive death. This full realisation did not dawn until after the resurrection.

For us who have lived all our lives on this side of the resurrection, it is easy to assume that we would give the same answer as Peter. We may do so, but going to the second stage is still a challenge. As Paul wrote to the Corinthians, the message of the cross seems like folly (1 Corinthians 1:18), and there are those in the church who find it hard to make sense of it. Jesus is easier to accept as a great moral teacher, or as a healer with remarkable powers, or as a prophet who showed us how to live, or simply as one of the great figures of history. In tough times we may wish he was more of a Jimmy Saville who could 'fix it' so that our dreams came true, or someone who would smite our enemies, or 'beam us up' out of conflict and chaos. Jesus does none of these things because they do not change our hearts. When later Jesus speaks to the people he explains what being a follower of his really means: 'Anyone who wants to be a follower of mine must renounce self; he must take up his cross and follow me. Whoever wants to save his life will lose it, but whoever loses his life for my sake and for the gospel's will save it.' This is a radical call, requiring a deep change of heart. It is also a clear statement that Jesus will not be the kind of Messiah that the people wanted. Instead Jesus calls his followers to regard their very life as forfeit, and to lose themselves in devotion to him and the gospel he proclaims. Paradoxically, those who lose themselves in this way will in fact find their true selves. This is a huge challenge, particularly in our culture which encourages us to do our own thing, where status and personal success come through acquisition and consumption, where the good news is to be up with the latest fashion, or the success of one's team in sport. Like Peter, I understand what it means, but really taking it into my life, allowing it to change my ideas and my lifestyle, does not come so easily.

Reflect today on how you really answer Jesus' question: 'And you, who do you say I am?' And what about losing your life for his sake and the gospel's?

2. A Glimpse of Glory

Read Mark 9:2-13

The story now moves from Jesus' teaching the people in public to a private episode with only the three disciples closest to Jesus. Mark is precise about the timing, thereby emphasising the significance of the event. It is 'six days later' that Jesus led Peter and James and John up a high mountain, and there in their presence he was transfigured. Precisely what happened it is impossible to know, but the experience was an overwhelming one of light, of clarity. The heavenly calling and destiny of Jesus shines forth, and the disciples are terrified and disoriented. Here is the sign from heaven that the Pharisees desired, but it is shown just to three people. Why? Because, as I have said above, signs are ambivalent; they will not convince the sceptical, who will always be able to rationalise them, or simply to ignore them. You can only see what you expect to see or are able to recognise. Signs speak to those whose eyes are already open, confirming and deepening their vision. Because of this, as they descend the mountain, Jesus instructs the three not to tell anyone else what they had seen.

Peter, James and John see Jesus as he truly is, surrounded by the divine glory. On either side are Moses and Elijah, representing the two pillars of the Jewish faith, the Law and the Prophets. Elijah is also the destined forerunner, the one who will come to set all things in order, preparing the way for the Messiah. (Jesus later explains that he has come – in the person of John the Baptist – but that he was not recognised, just as Jesus has not been recognised.) The vision is messianic, and confirms the truth of what Jesus has taught about his messiahship. The voice from heaven repeats the revelation at Jesus' baptism: 'This is my beloved Son; listen to him.' As his ministry drew to a close, God promised Moses that he would raise up for the people another prophet like him, one of their own: 'I shall put my words into his mouth. He will declare to them whatever I command him; if anyone refuses to listen to the words which he will speak in my name I shall call that person to account.' (Deuteronomy 18:18) Jesus is that prophet, the successor to Moses, who, like Moses, speaks the words of God. Listen to him!

The transfiguration was an event at the edge of experience, nevertheless it helps us to understand events within experience. Seeing the familiar in a new light is something that has happened to most of us. We see someone coping with adversity, or showing leadership or generosity, or displaying a 'hidden' talent, and we exclaim, 'I didn't know he had it in him! The person takes on a new quality in our eyes; they are, in a way, transfigured. In a similar way we may see a familiar view at dawn or sunset, or in the winter light, and it is as though we have not seen it before. It is shot through with light in a way that reveals new dimensions and perspectives. It is transfigured. There are also special moments in prayer or in worship, or listening to music, or looking at a work of art, when our spirit is lifted and God seems to have addressed us. The moment is transfigured. We cannot live at that level of intensity; like Jesus and the disciples we have to descend the mountain and resume our lives, and when we do so following him will not seem so easy. We need to 'listen' to these experiences for they are given to us as a sign of how things really are. In tough times, when faith is challenged and we feel more the absence than the presence of God, we need to go back to them and draw strength and encouragement from them. In times of dryness and doubt, testing and temptation, loneliness and suffering, we can re-live that moment of transfiguration and know again that God is real and Jesus is Lord. In his light we see light.

Think today about a special moment when God seemed very real for you. How have you drawn on that experience? Or perhaps you have had the experience and missed the meaning?

3. Only By Prayer
Read Mark 9:14-29 and 10:1-12

When Jesus returns from the mountain he finds the other disciples have been trying to cast out a demon but have failed. Earlier he had sent them out with authority over unclean spirits and they had returned and reported to him all that they had done. Presumably this included driving out spirits, but on this occasion they had not succeeded. As with the Pharisees who asked for a sign, Jesus' response has a note of exasperation: 'What an unbelieving generation! How long shall I be with you? Bring him to me.' When he sees the boy his tone softens and he asks his father how long he has suffered: it is from childhood. As the disciples have failed to heal him, his father seems unsure whether a

cure is possible. Jesus again is emphatic in his reply: 'If it is possible! Everything is possible to one who believes.' This evokes
one of the most moving responses in the gospels; the father cries
out in anguish: 'I believe; help my unbelief.' It is the cry of
Christians in every age, 'I have faith; help me where faith falls
short.' Jesus drives out the unclean spirit and raises the boy to
his feet. Mark omits the usual astonished response of the crowd;
instead he adds an after-note: when Jesus is asked privately by
the disciples why they could not cast out the demon, he replies
pithily, 'This kind cannot be driven out except by prayer.'

The two memorable sayings in this story, the father's haunt-
ing cry and Jesus' pithy reply, seem to belong together: both are
about depth in faith. Deep faith is not about believing the unbe-
lievable, but about enlarging the area of life that we let our belief
touch. This is another example of the difference between faith
and belief. Moving from belief to faith is like learning to live in
love. The excitement of falling in love, when we can hardly bear
to be separated from our beloved, must change into a deeper,
trustful relationship if we are to live and grow together. The
essence of this is a commitment, person to person, which en-
thrones the other not just in our desires but in our heart, so that
they become part of our being. This is to have faith in another
person. Mother Mary Clare describes faith in God in the same
way: 'Faith, as the Old Testament speaks of it, and as the saints
inspired by the New have experienced it, is total commitment,
person to person. It is more than reliance on mercy and forgiveness, or the most devoted admiration of the idealist. It must be a
response to the Divine Personality so that there is a knitting together of persons – the Lover and the Beloved.' (*Encountering the
Depths*, p 6) It is in this commitment that we begin to align ourselves with God so that his power flows through us and we can
be used by him to do his will.

'This kind cannot be driven out except by prayer.' Healing
depends more on the faith of the healer than on the faith of the
sufferer. Perhaps this story tells us that there are some conditions which are so acute, or where the evil is so deep-seated, that

only one whose life is deeply aligned with God can touch them. This seems to be the case in medicine; some doctors are able to bring about a cure in conditions where others cannot. This will often be because of greater skill, but sometimes it will also be because the physician has so given himself to his art (and healing is an art) that he is used in a way that others cannot be. (This may also help us to understand why in some conditions, despite faith, there is no cure.)

The disciples may have seen the truth about Jesus but they still have a way to go; their prayer has to be deeper, and this is not, as we might suppose, a matter of technique but of commitment. As you reflect today, think about prayer as commitment, person to person. Pray the prayer of the father in the story: 'I believe; help my unbelief,' knowing that you are asking Christ for a deeper relationship with him.

4. Camels and Needles
Read Mark 10:17-31
For the moment we leave the next passage and move to the story about the rich young man. Like any public figure many, many people must have come up to Jesus, but this encounter is one of the few that Mark has recorded. It is not just that its relevance transcends the ages; rather it is because it illustrates so well what it means to follow Christ. Mark sets the scene: as Jesus was setting out on a journey the young man ran up to him, knelt before him, and addressed him respectfully, 'Good Teacher ...' This was not the challenging behaviour of the Pharisees; this was someone who was eager, and in earnest. Mark says that as Jesus looked at him 'his heart warmed to him,' and who would not? Here was someone who had done well in life, whose faith was real, whose conduct was exemplary, but who felt that, despite all this, there was something missing. This encounter took place over two thousand years ago, but it has a very contemporary feel. Prosperity does not equate with happiness and fulfilment. We may, to use Harold Macmillan's famous phrase, have never had it so good, but equally we have never had it so empty. The

search for happiness and meaning in life is frenetic and un-requited.

Jesus' response is to tell the young man to keep the com-mandments, and the ones he names are significant because they are all to do with personal relationships, about being, not doing. What the young man seeks will be found there. 'But I've done all that since I was a boy,' the young man replies. There is no doubt-ing that he had, and there is left in the air the unspoken question, 'Why isn't it enough?' Jesus takes the matter deeper. Eternal life is not won through keeping the rules; righteousness demands more than goodness. What the young man seeks will only come through a deep change of heart. And with his deep insight into people Jesus speaks the word that will liberate the young man if he will hear it: 'One thing you lack. Go, sell everything you have, and give to the poor, and you will have treasure in heaven; then come and follow me.' The young man's face fell and he went away with a heavy heart; for he was a man of great wealth.

You do not have to have great wealth to feel as the young man did; modest possessions are enough to foster an attachment that is stronger than our attachment to God. The commitment of person to person, that Mother Mary Clare describes, must over-come a powerful god called 'materialism'. Jesus describes its grip in graphic terms: 'It is easier for a camel to pass through the eye of a needle than for a rich man to enter the kingdom of God.' Mark says the disciples 'were more astonished than ever,' and wondered if anyone could be saved. Jesus' imagery is so strongly drawn that in practice it tends to be ignored: he cannot be serious. And in any event has not modern economics confirmed that wealth, in the form of capital, is essential to fighting the very things that grind people down and imprison their spirits just as much as sin: things like dirty water, poor health care, lack of food, shelter and employment? Yes, it has; but Jesus does not condemn the right use of wealth; he condemns the way we come to depend upon it as a substitute for God. It is the place that the young man's possessions occupied in his heart that prevented him from gain-ing eternal life, not the mere fact that he was very rich.

Jesus told him to give to the poor. Our attitude towards the poor as well as towards our possessions also tells us where our heart is. Time and again the Bible places the poor, the widow and the stranger in a special category; they are especially beloved of God, and his people must also make them their special concern. This challenges not only the disposition of our hearts but also the adequacy of our economics. It is the state of the poor that determines the justice of an economic system, not the general level of prosperity. Personally and nationally, it is what we *are*, not what we have achieved, that has eternal value. Jesus tells the rich young man that at the gate of heaven he can take through only what he possesses within himself. Gaining eternal life is nothing to do with what he owns or what he has achieved, and it will be only through the grace of God for whom all things are possible. In the end, the rich, like the poor, must depend on the mercy of God. In the midst of this challenge there is encouragement: of all the people in the gospel, the rich young man is the only person whom Mark says Jesus loved. He loved the one person who desired to be close, who tried hard but who, nevertheless, failed. Failure does not cut us off from God: that is the good news.

This story is a telling illustration of all that Jesus has taught about discipleship: what is most important is where our hearts are fixed. We sin for the most part because we place our relationship with the things of God above our relationship with God himself. The question is not, 'What more can I do?', but, 'What more can I become?' in order to inherit eternal life. As you reflect on this story, imagine yourself in the position of the young man running up to Jesus: What would Jesus have said to you? What 'one thing' do you lack? Are you happy to be a failure whom Jesus loves?

5. Who is the Greatest?
Read Mark 9:30-50; 10:13-16 and 32-45
Today we bring together two passages in which Jesus teaches the disciples about his destiny in Jerusalem: that he will be

handed over into the power of men, who will kill him; and that three days later he will rise again. He has, of course, said this before at Caesarea Philippi; they did not understand then and they do not understand now, and they are afraid to ask. This is a very human touch: so often we feel we ought to know something, especially if it has been explained to us before, and we are afraid to ask for fear of appearing stupid. The extent of their misunderstanding is shown, first, by their argument about who was the greatest and, secondly, by James and John asking Jesus to do them a favour. In both cases it is an all-too-human concern for status.

In the first instance Jesus re-directs their ambition by talking about service. Service is the path to greatness: 'If anyone wants to be first, he must make himself last of all and servant of all.' As he said about the rich young man, things are ordered differently in the kingdom: 'many who are first will be last, and the last first.' Jesus makes his meaning clear by taking a child and setting him in front of them, and putting his arm around him. They must be willing to serve the least, like this child; and whoever does so will receive him, Jesus; and not only him, they will receive God himself. Whoever receives the least receives the greatest. On other occasions, too, Jesus reached out to those whom society despised; he touched the untouchable, the lepers, the tax collectors and sinners. The touch of Christ is a touch that reaches out and includes; it defined the community whom his followers were called to serve.

The same lesson is repeated when James and John ask if they can have the places of honour in the kingdom, one on his right and the other on his left. The request is made as they approach Jerusalem, and Mark records that the disciples were filled with awe; a sense of fear pervaded the group. When Jesus points out that to share his glory they must first share his fate, the two brothers say bravely that they will do so; but, not surprisingly, when the others hear of their request they are indignant. So Jesus explains again that in the kingdom honour is not bestowed as it is on earth: 'You know that among the Gentiles the recog-

nised rulers lord it over their subjects, and make their authority
felt. It shall not be so with you; among you whoever wants to be
first must be the slave of all. For the Son of Man did not come to
be served but to serve, and to give his life as a ransom for many.'
The willingness of James and John to drink the same cup as
Jesus will drink will not bring special status, for it is no more
than is asked of any disciple. With God there are no favours, no
special deals.

In both these episodes Jesus reverses the values common in
the world, and points to himself as the new source of value.
Because he has come to serve and give his life as a ransom for
many, this now becomes the supreme value among his followers. And because this is the way of God himself, it must also be
the supreme value for the world. There are, of course, many examples of selfless service inspired by the example of Christ, or
simply by our common humanity, from those who care for sick
and aged relatives to those who work tirelessly for justice and
peace. But service is not what comes to mind as the supreme
value in a world preoccupied by status, money, image and
celebrity. Those we are offered as rôle models – music, screen
and media personalities, sports professionals and self-made mil-
lionaires – often seem self-serving, and their affairs petty and
without moral substance. There are notable exceptions, but generally it seems that social responsibility does not come with the
riches they acquire. This is compounded by a popular culture
that is assertive, in-your-face, disrespectful and blame-averse,
and where rights come before responsibilities. By contrast Jesus
teaches a way of humility.

Humility comes from the Latin *humus*, meaning earth.
Humility is about being earthed, being in touch with the source
of our being. Humility is not a weak thing – always putting
yourself down – but an inner strength that comes from a true ap-
preciation of your place before God and within the community;
a strength that means that you do not have to have your own
way all the time. Humility is the foundation of love, the willingness to put the needs of others first – near and far away, to learn

from them, to serve them, and to suffer for them. Humility helps us to achieve an inner freedom that frees us from selfish impulses and allows us to be shaped by other people's lives. Jesus gives a lovely example of humility when he says that we need to be able to accept the kingdom of God like a child, that is with a trusting heart, happy to follow even though we do not know where the journey will end. It is hard for us to appreciate just how radical it was to use a child in this way. We are accustomed to children having rights; in Jesus' day they had no rights; they were like slaves, utterly without status. Yet it is the child, the one without status, without skills, a nobody, that Jesus embraces; a sign of how differently things are ordered in the kingdom. As Jesus said, the first will be last and the last first: humility is the way of the cross.

Humility is the salt that Jesus says we must have within ourselves. Reflect today on the virtue of humility: How far do you allow your self, your inner being, to be shaped by other people's lives, both those you know personally and those you know from the news – the needy as well as the needless?

6. Leaving Self Behind
Read Mark 10:46-52

Mark ends this section with the story of Bartimaeus, the man who has lost his sight. He cries out to Jesus, 'Son of David, have pity on me.' Jesus calls him and asks what he wants him to do for him, and Bartimaeus says, 'I want my sight back.' Jesus restores his sight, and he follows him in the way. The story encapsulates all that Mark has narrated so far. His generation have lost sight of God, and they lack that generosity of spirit which would enable them to follow trustfully in the way of faith. Now seeing clearly, Bartimaeus steps out into the way leaving his old, blind self behind. The section began with Jesus teaching the disciples that following in the way meant taking up their cross, and being prepared to lose their life for his sake, and the sake of the gospel. Only that way would they gain life, by which he meant life in communion with God, eternal life. It is a prize worth any sacrifice, and as I read this part of the gospel I am struck again and again by the strength of the language Jesus uses to impress this upon his hearers. It is perhaps strongest at the end of chapter nine, where he says that it is better to lose a hand, a foot, or an eye than to miss entering into eternal life. These words are a graphic image of leaving self behind, and of the pain of doing so, in order to enter the kingdom.

Leaving self behind means doing battle both with the gods of the age and the demons within.

The gods of the age are the accepted ways of doing things, the ideas that give life meaning, the goals that motivate us, the moral rules that guide us. The rich young man was living according to the gods of the age, at least as understood by the Pharisees. Not only was he scrupulously keeping the law, he also regarded himself as blessed because the Pharisees taught that riches and the responsibilities that they brought were a sign of God's favour. By and large we do not notice the gods of the age because we grow up under their tutelage; doing what is generally accepted is what seems natural and right. As the American theologian Walter Wink has observed, the gods incarnate themselves in the structures of society, and today those gods have an economic character, and our modern culture is an economic culture. 'The language of economics is the language through which the world is understood, the language by which human and social problems are defined and by which solutions to those problems are expressed. Our lives are dominated by the rituals of "getting and spending".' (Jane Collier, *Contemporary culture and the role of economics*, p 103) Economics expresses the spirit of the age. Economic theory, as a way of understanding and channelling human motivation, is based on the premise that conduct is determined by the rational pursuit of self-interest – that is taking self with you, not leaving self behind. Part of the reason for the widespread feelings of apathy and frustration today is that the economic view is a limited view, but has, nevertheless, become the dominant view; the economic model of human society has displaced the broader social model that underlies it. 'The drive for more and more material goods is a pre-occupying concern for economic activity. It justifies an accep-tance of a certain way of doing things, of particular lifestyles, which, *prima facie*, conflict with logic or with a sensible view of wider social goals. It leads to an acceptance of value systems which dictate action, or impose subservience, in a way that con-flicts with wider perceptions of social behaviour.' (Owen Nankivell, *Economics, Society and Values*, p 73)

Jesus was not the political leader of popular expectation, but that does not mean that his teaching has no political implic-ations. To place service, especially of the poorest, above all other values is to make demands on us not just individually, but as a nation and as a family of nations; and those demands are sacrifi-cial, part of the process of taking up our cross. To be true to the gospel we have to take the personal into the political. So down the ages, and particularly in our own time, Christians have worked tirelessly to challenge the structures of society in order to bring justice to the poor. A recent example of this was the campaign led by Jubilee 2000 to remit the debts of the world's poorest nations. The limited success so far achieved shows just how tight is the grip of the gods of the age. It also shows that these gods have to be fought, not propitiated, if the least are to be served as well as the great.

The personal challenge is to fight the demons within. They are all those selfish impluses, many deeply hidden within our psyche, that blind our sight and lead us astray – in other words, the causes of our sinfulness. At one level fighting the demons is simply a matter of getting our priorities right. Mark illustrates this with the question about divorce. Jesus refuses to deal with it at the level of rules – the level at which the Pharisees sought to test him. Rules, he says, are for those intent on having their own way. Instead he directs attention to the God-given purpose of marriage. Get that right, he says, and live by it. This, of course, is easier said than done, and so we need a way in which we can move to a deeper level where God's priorities take root in our hearts and we learn to live on his wavelength. This, really, is why we pray. Prayer is tuning-in to God before it is asking things of God, and the more we do this the better we see the demons within. In prayer we discover within ourselves the same roots of violence, frustration, despair and so on that we see in the world. Recognising them, we can hold them 'steadily to the only thing that can redeem them – the love of God.' (Mother Mary Clare, *Encountering the Depths*, p 11) Naming the demons within deprives them of power, and we gain in inner strength, or virtue.

Leaving self behind is to pursue the path of virtue. We do not hear much about virtue these days. Virtue has been replaced by values in today's world, but the two are not the same. Virtue has something given about it, an objective quality which values do not have. In our modern way we like to think that we choose our values, though in practice they are provided by the gods of the age. Our values express our lifestyle, the qualities and ethical standards we chose to live by. They are not, of course, all self-serving, but the point is that they are *my* values; values come from *me*. Virtue, by contrast, is an inner quality, a grace that enables us to conform our being to the truth, to live a life that is morally pleasing to God. Virtue is God-given; it is part of the light that comes from God himself. Virtue accepts that God has determined the qualities and ethical standards that enable us to live a true human life, and it gives us the inner strength to live by those qualities and standards, particularly when they are altruistic: these are God's values. Virtue is not concerned so much with lifestyle as with life-giving style. Virtue comes from God. Perhaps the time has come to be more single-minded and let virtue shape our values.

V

Challenge and Confrontation
Chapters 11-13

Introduction

Mark now begins his account of the final week of Jesus' life. The week falls into two parts, Jesus' entry into Jerusalem and his challenge to the authorities, and his arrest, death and resurrection. The story of God coming among his people to redeem them now reaches its climax, and that climax begins with a confrontation.

Like Christmas, Holy Week suffers from familiarity; we know the story, and we are not really alert to the differences in the way that it is told in the four gospels. This is a shame because each evangelist tells the story from a different perspective, bringing out aspects that are not found in the other gospels, and emphasising his own special understanding of who Jesus is. Once I asked the different members of a home group each to read just one gospel; when asked for their impressions one person said he had been struck by how much of the story was not there! Our experience of Holy Week, as with Christmas, tends to be a conflation of the four versions: nowhere is this clearer than with the seven 'words' from the cross. In fact Mark and Matthew give just one word, 'My God, my God, why have you forsaken me?' Luke gives another three: 'Father, forgive them; they do not know what they are doing'; 'Truly, I tell you: today you will be with me in Paradise'; and 'Father, into your hands I commit my spirit', and omits the one in Mark and Matthew. John gives a further three, again omitting those in Mark, Matthew and Luke: 'Mother, there is your son'; 'I thirst'; and 'It is finished.' It is useless to ask whether Jesus said all seven, and if so, in which order. The 'words' given by each evangelist reflect their individual understanding of the story, and if we want to let each unique voice speak to us, we have to try to put out of our minds the 'words' and the other parts of the story that they miss out. This is especially true for Mark whose account of the passion is stark compared with the other gospels.

The note of conflict in Mark's gospel is unremitting; from first to last Jesus challenges the scribes and the Pharisees, and when he is not confronting them he is taking the disciples to task for their failure to understand his teaching. Mark has none of the 'softer' stories of the other gospels, as for example the parable of the Prodigal Son in Luke. Nor is there any teaching about the love of God; that is, of course, implicit in the picture of the suffering Son of Man, and in Jesus' table fellowship, for example, but it is not developed. Mark's concern is to emphasise the radical newness of all that Jesus was and taught, a newness that challenged the religious foundations of Israel.

So Jesus comes at last to the Temple, the symbol of both the Jewish faith and the Jewish nation, and the passion that he has thrice predicted begins. His entry into Jerusalem was no spur of the moment happening. Jesus had arranged for a colt to be available for him so that he could act out the prophecy of Zechariah who foretold that the Lord would come to his Temple riding on a colt, the foal of a donkey (Zechariah 9:9). Kings rode on a donkey when they came in peace. While this may be the message intended by Jesus, it cannot be other than a provocation, especially when it is followed the next day by the cleansing of the temple. The religious authorities demand an explanation but, characteristically, Jesus declines to give a straight answer, and instead adds to the provocation by telling the parable of the Vineyard against them. The point of the parable is very clear, and the authorities know that it was aimed at them. The challenge has turned into condemnation; they cannot allow it to continue or their authority will be completely undermined. At the beginning of his gospel Mark said that they began to plot how they might bring about his death. So far they have not been able to touch him because his popularity has protected him; but his challenge is getting too close to home; they must try again to condemn him with his own words, or resort to some other means.

As Mark describes the confrontation, each of the main religious groups in turn attempts to trap him: the priests and the scribes, the Pharisees and the Herodians, and the Sadducees. Each poses a question, and each is rebuffed. Here we see Jesus in control; the questions are not so much answered as refuted. In the end all the parties are silenced, and their double standards exposed. From the opening of the gospel until now Mark has presented Jesus as the one who set the agenda, but this will soon change. Anticipating this, the section concludes in chapter 13 with a series of solemn warnings to the disciples. As we shall see, there are grounds for thinking that these words, or some of them, were not actually spoken by Jesus, but even so, the disciples could be in no doubt that a cataclysm was upon them. A final conflict is inevitable, the only question is whether Jesus was right when he said that it would end with his death.

1. Hosanna!
Read Mark 11:1-11
The entry into Jerusalem is the event for which Jesus has long prepared his disciples, and for which Mark has prepared his readers. He makes it clear that Jesus carefully prepared his entry, and that a clear message was being conveyed. It is, in effect, an enacted parable. This is evident from the arrangements for the collecting of the colt, and from the fact that Jesus came mounted into the Holy City unlike the pilgrims who traditionally approached on foot. Jesus was no ordinary pilgrim. Mark's account also assumes an awareness of what would have been in the minds of the people. It was the time of the Passover and nationalistic feelings would have been strong; the annual remembrance of the time when God liberated them from slavery in Egypt made real their hope that God would again liberate them from subjection. Jesus chose to arrive by descending from the Mount of Olives which, in popular belief, would be associated with the coming of the Messiah. They would also have been familiar with the prophecy of Zechariah:

Daughter of Zion rejoice with all your heart;
shout in triumph, daughter of Jerusalem!
See, your king is coming to you,
his cause won, his victory gained,
humble and mounted on a donkey,
on a colt, the foal of a donkey. (Zechariah 9:9)

Jesus' entry is the enactment of this prophecy and, for those with eyes to see, a clear confirmation of all that he has taught so far about his messiahship. He was not the warrior-messiah of popular expectation, but the Son of Man who came in peace. His mount is actually a colt 'which no one has ever yet ridden,' a sign of newness that underlines the new thing that God is about to do through him.

Other details too are important. Jesus is accompanied by his followers; Mark does not have the crowds that are present in Matthew's and John's accounts (Matthew 21:8; John 12:12). Mark says 'those in front and those behind shouted,' not the crowds; and the shout does not describe Jesus as 'king of Israel,' as in John, or 'king,' as in Luke (19:38), but 'he who comes in the name of the Lord!' and 'Blessed is the kingdom of our father David which is coming!' Mark, who is writing nearer the events than any of the other evangelists, does not describe the great spectacle of John who says that 'the great crowd of pilgrims who had come to the festival ... went out to meet him with palm branches in their hands.' (John 12:12, 13) Instead in his account it is much smaller event, composed of Jesus and his followers. In modern terms it would have looked more like a small peace march than a mass demonstration. As Mark describes it, Jesus' entry into Jerusalem was certainly nothing like a popular uprising, and that perhaps is why it aroused no attention from the authorities. In the eyes of the Romans Jesus posed no threat to public order. In Mark's story the crowds of our imagination are simply not there, yet to those who were there the meaning of what Jesus did was clear.

Looking back on these events two millennia later, with the knowledge of what that small beginning led to, it is natural to assume that in his day Jesus attracted the vast crowds that have assembled in his name since then, like the million young people who met Pope Benedict XVI at Cologne in 2005. But that, according to Mark, is not how it was. In his account of the passion Jesus is an isolated figure, and this may help us to be realistic about our expectations of the Church. In 1998 I attended the biggest Christian gathering I have experienced, the second European Ecumenical Assembly at Graz in Austria. Around 10,000 Christians from all churches and denominations travelled from all over Europe, and the week we spent together was a wonderful experience. But, looking back, I wonder just how many of the ordinary people of Graz were aware that anything special was taking place in their midst, and if they did whether they were in fact that interested. Just like the crowds in Jerusalem. There are those who look forward to the Church becoming again the force it was in the Middle Ages, but I am not sure that that will happen, nor that it is what we should expect or want to happen. Established religion loses its cutting edge, and those countries where governments have been formed by 'Christian' parties have ended up looking like any other modern state. Mark's message is clear, religion takes root in the spirit; you 'see' the truth from the signs that confront you, and if you do not, then the truth will pass you by. You cannot force-feed people with the truth. So as Jesus enters Jerusalem, his followers point out to those who will hear the truth of what they see, but most do not have ears to hear, and the truth passes them by. The Church must proclaim the truth, but it must not expect to fare better than Jesus did.

Reflect today on the way St Mark tells the story of 'Palm Sunday', and take to heart his particular understanding.

2. No Figs! No Trade!
Read Mark 11:12-25

In Matthew and Luke the accounts of the entry into Jerusalem, the cleansing of the Temple and the dispute with the religious authorities comprise one continuous narrative, but Mark breaks it up so that it occurs over three days, and within it he inserts the story of the fig tree. This is a difficult story, probably the most difficult in the gospels. Cursing a fig tree for having no fruit when it is not the season for figs seems completely unreasonable and, more importantly, quite out of character for Jesus. Nor indeed does it provide a very edifying example of faith in the power of prayer to achieve what the believer asks. Faith may be able to move mountains (a figurative expression used then much as we use it today), but surely not everything that the believer wants, if he truly believes that he has received it, will be his, particularly if it is akin to cursing a tree. One conjecture is that the story was originally a parable – it is told in this form by Luke (Luke 13:6-9) – which somehow or other became associated with a withered fig tree that Jesus was believed to have cursed on his way to Jerusalem. Whatever its origins, by placing it where he does Mark sees it as interpreting Jesus' actions in the Temple. The fate of the fig tree symbolised the fate that awaited the Jewish people and the temple. 'Like the fig tree with its leaves, the Jewish people made a fine show with their numerous ceremonies and outward observances, but when the Messiah came looking for the fruit of righteousness he found none, and the result was condemnation and destruction for Judaism as it was for the tree.' (Denis Nineham, *St Mark*, p 299)

From this, Mark's understanding of the cleansing of the temple is clear, and it follows from all that he has told us about Jesus' continual dispute with the Pharisees. The temple stands for the Jewish people and religion and there is something rotten at its heart, so much so, that radical action is called for. All the practices that have arisen and corrupted its life must be cleared away and a fresh start made. Like his entry into Jerusalem, his actions enact prophecy, this time of God's final intervention in history. Zechariah had foretold that on the day of the Lord 'no longer will any trader be seen in the house of the Lord of Hosts.' (Zechariah 14:21) Jesus also refers to two other prophecies as he clears out the traders and their customers. Isaiah had foretold that the Lord would welcome gentiles who gave their allegiance to him: 'Their offerings and sacrifices will be acceptable on my altar; for my house shall be called a house of prayer for all nations.' (Isaiah 56:7) And Jeremiah had condemned those whose actions were wrong – oppressing the alien, the fatherless, and the widow, acting criminally, and worshipping other gods – who nevertheless came to the temple and worshipped as though they were guiltless. 'Do you regard this house which bears my name as a bandits' cave?' says the Lord, 'I warn you, I myself have seen all this.' (Jeremiah 7:1-11) The radical action required is to be open to other nations, allowing the gentiles proper access to the temple (the trading took place in the Court of the Gentiles thereby depriving them of their rightful place), and true repentance, so that worship is in spirit and in truth, and does not degenerate into a mere outward observance.

The situation in the temple was typical of the problems that arise when religion and the state become too closely identified. On the one hand it becomes exclusive; if you are not a member of the national community you cannot be a member of the religious community. Apartheid was perhaps the worst example of this, but we also see it in less institutionalised forms of social and racial exclusion. On the other hand worship degenerates into formalism: no real repentance, that is a deep turning to God, is required. The important thing is that you live up to expectations, and if that includes attending worship then so be it, but the heart is not engaged. We see these tendencies in Islam as well as Christianity, with butchers like Saddam Hussein attending the mosque and terrorists in Northern Ireland going to church. The result of exclusivity and formalism is not just a corrupt institution but a wrong picture of God, and that has been a consistent theme of Jesus' teaching. In the public sphere the Church does its work best when it functions as a kind of loyal opposition, as it did during the Falklands War. It serves the best interests of the state not when it blesses state policy come what may, but when it reminds that state of its moral basis and of the wider interests that it should serve. When Jesus came to Jerusalem and drove the traders out of the temple this is what he was doing. He showed that he came in peace, but peace depends on the presence of justice, morality and right relationships.

This episode focuses a consistent theme in Mark's gospel, the disturbing and challenging character of much of what Jesus said and did. His picture is far removed from the 'gentle Jesus' of childhood. Reflect today on this disturbing figure who resorted to violent action; is this part of your picture of Jesus?

3. By What Authority?
Read Mark 11:27-12:12

Jesus may not have led a mass movement, but he attracted much popular interest and could not be ignored. However, his popularity meant that the Jewish religious authorities had to be cautious in the way they dealt with him. The cleansing of the temple was a direct challenge and a response was required; his popularity meant that that they could not arrest him, so a delegation from the Sanhedrin (who were responsible for the temple police) was sent to question him. The issue is authority, as it generally is for those in charge: 'By what authority are you acting like this? Who gave you authority to act in this way?' The question was hardly a polite enquiry, and was designed to make the point that, in fact, Jesus had no authority. He replies with a standard rabbinical response, a counter-question designed to settle the issue: 'The baptism of John: was it from God, or from men?' The question goes to the heart of the matter, but avoids focusing on Jesus himself. The authorities accepted John as a prophet, and of course his authority did not come from them; Jesus is inviting them to admit that in John they recognised that God was at work. It would follow, of course, that God was also at work in Jesus as his works were greater than John's. In refusing to answer they admit that they cannot recognise God's action; that destroys their claim to authority and, therefore, their right to interrogate Jesus. He declines to state his authority, and this response is consistent with his parables and miracles; in effect he says, 'If you cannot see it, then nothing will be achieved by telling you.' The truth has to come from the heart.

Jesus then drives the point home with the parable of the vineyard. The vineyard was a common metaphor in love poetry, and
Isaiah had used it to symbolise Israel. His story of the vineyard
tells of Israel's failure to produce the fruits of righteousness despite God's care and protection. So God abandons his vineyard
and it becomes a wasteland. 'He looked for justice but found
bloodshed, for righteousness but heard cries of distress.' (Isaiah
5:1-7; Psalm 80 uses the same image.) John Robinson suggested
that originally the parable had just two sets of servants sent to
reclaim the vineyard, and such a version is found in the apoc-
ryphal *Gospel of Thomas* (John Robinson, *Can We Trust the New
Testament?*, pp 55, 56). The two sets of servants correspond to the
two waves of prophets – in the eighth and sixth centuries BC –
sent to call Israel back to God. The message of the parable is beyond doubt and the authorities know that it is aimed at them:
they have not listened to the prophets; they have failed to bring
forth from Israel the fruits of righteousness; they have not been
able to recognise the Messiah in their midst; their authority is at
an end.

Perhaps we ought to spare a thought for the leaders of Israel.
Leadership is a fraught enterprise; on the one hand the leaders
carry the expectations of the people, and on the other hand they
are constrained by what is possible, and an element in that con-
straint is a popular dislike of radical change. The people want it
both ways, and popular demands will often be for a short-term
remedy and may sit light to the requirements of law and morality.
Leadership requires wisdom and moral strength, but these are
not the qualities that always go hand-in-hand with powerful
personalities and popular acclaim. And power once gained is
hard to relinquish, as we see with so many autocratic leaders in
the world, and the powerful tend to enlarge the matters and the
resources they control. As one of the early American Presidents,
James Madison, observed, power is of an encroaching nature, or
in Lord Acton's famous phrase, 'power tends to corrupt, and absolute power corrupts absolutely.' (Lord Acton in a letter to
Bishop Mandell Creighton: Louise Creighton (ed), *The Life and*

Letters of Mandell Creighton) Corrupt religious leadership is doubly pernicious because it sets itself to serve a higher interest. Christian leadership has a threefold character, it is pastoral, priestly and prophetic, and within the prophetic rôle is the duty of equipping people to recognise the hand of God in the world. This, according to Mark, is what the leaders of Israel had consistently failed to do.

As you reflect on this encounter, ask what you expect of both secular and religious leaders and pray that they may have wisdom and moral strength.

4. Mite not Might
Read Mark 12:13-44

After the priests and the scribes two more groups come forward to challenge Jesus, the Pharisees (making common cause on this occasion with the Herodians, whom they normally opposed) and the Sadducees. Both groups were hostile to Jesus, the Sadducees to the point of hatred. They wished to arrest him, but feared to do so because Jesus remained popular with the people. If his popularity could be weakened by trapping him in his own words, their task would be easier; so they come to question him with malice in their hearts.

The Pharisees' question raises the legitimacy of paying the Roman poll tax, a hated exaction that provoked riots when it was introduced. The question is obviously a trap, and Jesus responds, 'Why are you trying to catch me out?' If he replies, 'Yes, pay the poll tax,' he would lose much of his popular support; if he says, 'No, don't pay,' he can be denounced to the Romans as a rebel, and they would arrest him. Jesus' response is masterly, and, as Mark says, leaves them 'completely taken aback'. In cold print his reply reads like a judicious, even-handed statement, but this is unlikely, given the way that Jesus has responded in the past. The second clause would have been emphasised over the first clause: 'Pay Caesar what belongs to Caesar, *and God what belongs to God*.' Coinage was regarded as the property of the emperor in whose name it circulated. In effect Jesus says,

their first duty, of returning Ceasar's coinage to him, is insignifi-
cant compared to their second duty, of honouring God in their
hearts.

The Sadducees were the high-priestly aristocracy, conserv-
ative in their views, rejecting new ideas like angels and spirits
and the resurrection of the dead which the Pharisees accepted.
(All these beliefs were of recent origin at the time, and Jesus
clearly accepted them, agreeing with the Pharisees.) Their question was a well-known joke that was going the rounds at the
time, designed to show that the resurrection from the dead was
a ludicrous idea. The Sadducees are told straight that they do
not know what they are talking about – and this is the establishment! The life to come, says Jesus, is not a heavenly version of
life on earth, and the Bible itself witnessed to life after death.
(Perhaps we should note in passing that the first part of the
answer does not support popular ideas today about being re-
united with our loved ones in the life to come. But that is another
story.)

The two parties fail to undermine Jesus, a failure driven
home by the story of the scribe, one of the religious lawyers,
who warmly agrees with Jesus. His words echo the words of the
prophets that God is more concerned with the state of our hearts
than the formal observance of religious obligations. Putting the
love of God and the love of neighbour at the head of the list of
commandments means that all the elaborate casuistry beloved
of the establishment, like the 'corban' law that Jesus criticised
(7:9-13), is swept aside. The lawyer agrees, and says that the
whole Jewish sacrificial system is nothing compared to personal
devotion to God and Man. Jesus commends him, 'You are not
far from the kingdom of God.' Mark follows this with a warning
about the hypocrisy of the leaders, and the story of the widow's
mite. The contrast is masterly, and illustrates all that Jesus has
said and taught. The widow from her meagre resources gives
sacrificially to God; her heart is in the right place; her worship is
true. Those who seek the places of honour at feasts and the chief
seats in the synagogues, who dress in long robes to draw atten-

tion to their position, may give more, but in the sight of God it is worth less. The widow has shown a generosity of heart that is sadly lacking in the powerful. Not only has Jesus escaped their trap and refuted their questions, he has accused the leaders of hypocrisy and exposed them as hard-hearted. Unlike them he will give himself wholly to God and for the people as the widow has given her mite.

Like the widow, the poor often show greater generosity than the rich. They know that we sink or swim together, a fact that wealth, even modest wealth, allows us to overlook. Following Jesus is about giving our whole heart to him and not about contributing to a cause. Jesus said, 'Where your treasure is, there will your heart be also.' (Luke 12:34) As you reflect today, ask yourself how whole-hearted is your commitment to Jesus. Where is your treasure laid up?

5. Be Alert!

Read Mark 13

This section ends with a series of warnings about the End, the time of judgement, which Jesus expected to happen soon after his death. Chapter 13 is known as 'the little apocalypse', and this reflects the style of the writing which is found in other parts of the Bible, for example, the Book of Daniel and the Revelation of John. 'Apocalypse' means 'unveiling' or 'revelation'; it is a literary genre designed to reveal the hidden purposes of God. It appears to predict the future, but in fact it is a commentary on current events designed to show that the suffering of the faithful will not go unnoticed by God, and that out of their affliction will come their vindication. In the end, though they cannot see it now, God will defeat their enemies. The aside remark 'Let the reader understand,' supports this interpretation. It only makes sense if it refers to an event within the experience of the reader. 'The abomination of desolation' echoes Daniel's words about an idol that would be set up in the temple desecrating the holy place (Daniel 11:31 and 12:11), and may well refer to the statue of himself that the Emperor Caligula tried to set up in the temple in

AD 40. If this is so, then this passage must post-date Jesus' ministry and cannot have been spoken by him. The whole chapter
has a different feel to the rest of the gospel, and seems to have
been composed by Mark from collections of material that were
available to him, some of which may come from Jesus.

There are also problems in taking it literally. It clearly pre-
dicts an imminent end-time, and that did not occur and has not
occurred since. If the events described – wars and rumours of
wars, earthquakes and famines, the sun and the moon darkened,
and stars falling from the sky – are the signs of the End, 'the
birth pangs of the new age', then there can scarcely have been a
period in history when the signs were not fulfilled. Time and
again, there have been wars and distress on earth and strange
signs in the heavens, but the End has not come. These signs are
clearly fulfilled today, but the End has not come. So how are we
to understand this chapter?

The 'End' that the Bible refers to is the completion of God's
purposes, which was expected to be a time of judgement, and at
the time would have been thought of as the end of the world.
Modern science tells us how the world is likely to end, in a grad-
ual cooling of the planet over very many years. Today we have
to separate the two ends. When the two are confused, because of
the human capacity for violence, we tended to think of the End
as violent, a cataclysm. But if God is a God of love we cannot
imagine that he would wish to destroy his creation, the work
and object of his love; rather he would wish to save it from destruction. The End God has in view, according to the Lord's
Prayer, is that his kingdom shall come on earth as in heaven. The
End that God purposes will be a time of fulfilment and not destruction. We cannot know precisely what form the End will
take, but we can be sure that it will not be less than a work of
love. But a work of love can be disturbing. As Malachi puts it,
'Who can endure the day of his coming? Who can stand firm
when he appears? (Malachi 3:2) The coming of God cannot be
other than a time of upheaval. As Mark has shown throughout
his gospel, the coming of Jesus was a huge upheaval. The ap-

pearance of goodness is a time of judgement; it cannot be otherwise. This is so in every age, and so it is bound to be the case that
the signs are always and everywhere fulfilled. The End is now
and always: it is the challenge to faith and obedience that Jesus
preached, and which his followers must preach in his name.
And they too will experience the opposition and the condemnation that he experienced, so it is right that just before the final
act of his ministry Jesus warns them to be alert.

Removing the coded language, there remains much in this
chapter that is within the experience of Christians both down
the ages and today. So as Jesus says, we must be on our guard,
alert to read the signs of the times. We must expect to be held to
account for our faith, opposed, derided, ridiculed and even per-
secuted, but at such times we can be sure that God will put the
words we need in our mouths. We must pray for one another
and also that God's purposes, the completion of his work, will
be fulfilled. We must also learn from the conviction of the first
Christians that behind the events we see and which disturb us,
God is at work ensuring that the final outcome will be good and
not evil. The End will be God's.

Think today about all that Jesus has said and done, particularly in the few days covered in this week's readings, and reflect
on what that would mean for the disciples after his death. How
would they be treated; with what challenges would they be
faced? Are there parallels today in the life of the church, and in
the lives of individual Christians?

6. Judgement and Redemption

In exile in Babylon the prophet Ezekiel denounced the leaders of
Israel who cared only for themselves and not for the flock. The
sheep were scattered on the hills, ravaged by wild beasts, with
no one to go in search of them. To the leaders, 'The Lord God
says: I am against the shepherds and shall demand from them
an account of my sheep. I shall dismiss them from tending my
flock: no longer will they care only for themselves; I shall rescue
my sheep from their mouths, and they will feed on them no

more. Now I myself shall take thought for my sheep and search for them.' (Ezekiel 34:10, 11) In cleansing the temple and in rebuking the leaders of Israel Jesus delivered the judgement of God prophesied by Ezekiel. In and through the Son of Man God has taken thought for his sheep, gone in search of them and brought them home. But this will cost the Son no less than his life. Suffering is an inescapable part of redemption. It means 'buying back', and the price has to be paid.

Suffering is also an inescapable part of judgement. The Exile to Babylon during which Ezekiel lived was understood by the prophets as the price Israel paid for forsaking the Lord. It was a time of personal and communal tribulation and religious upheaval. Ezekiel lived through 'the greatest catastrophe and transformation the religion of Israel had ever experienced: the transition from a religion identified with a land and a temple, with its sacrifices, to a religion identified with a community of people, thus leading ultimately to the full development of the synagogue where the study of law is paramount, the essential Judaism of today.' (Preface to the Book of Ezekiel in *The Oxford Study Bible*, REB version, p 857) The worship of the temple was re-instituted when the Israelites were restored to the land under Nehemiah, but the study of law as the foundation of religion continued to be the defining influence in the faith. The result was the elaborate and legalistic religion that itself was in need of transformation. Not only was it failing to feed the spirits of the people, its conception of God was wrong, the inevitable consequence of religion becoming too formal in its ritual, too concerned with the maintenance of tradition in its teaching, too cerebral in its expression, and too identified with the state or nation. In other words, it loses its spirit. Jesus came to inaugurate another religious transformation, a renewal of the spirit, which Ezekiel had also foretold. 'I shall give you a new heart and put a new spirit within you; I shall remove the heart of stone from your body and give you a heart of flesh. I shall put my spirit within you and make you conform to my statutes; you will observe my laws faithfully.' (Ezekiel 36:26, 27)

Judgement and redemption are two sides of the same coin. 'Say to the anxious, "Be strong, fear not, your God is coming with judgement, coming with judgement to save you".' (Isaiah 35:4) God's judgement is not aimed at condemnation but at reconciliation. As John wrote, 'It was not to judge the world that God sent his Son into the world, but that through him the world might be saved.' (John 3:17) Judgement goes against the spirit of the age, with its permissive morality and refusal of responsibility; we are happier with reconciliation. But you cannot have the one without the other. It is because we reject the idea of judgement that we fail to recognise God's presence in the world today. When asked whether God was present in the world today, Archbishop Michael Ramsay responded that he was present in judgement, and spoke of 'three boils', three profound moral issues that faced the world: the proliferation of arms, the spread of racial hatred, and the division between rich and poor. Were he writing today he would surely have added a fourth, global warming and pollution. God is present to us in these issues, confronting us, as Jesus confronted the leaders of Israel, with the meanness of our spirit that allows these boils to go on festering. If we complain of God's absence, it is simply that our pride obscures his presence. 'When men and nations turn away from God's laws and prefer the courses dictated by pride and selfishness to the courses dictated by conscience, calamitous results follow. God is not absent from the contemporary scene; he is present, present in judgement through the catastrophes that follow human wilfulness. And nowhere is the divine judgement as the working out of human folly put more trenchantly than in the words of the Psalmist: "So he gave them their heart's desire, and sent leanness withal into their souls".' (Michael Ramsay, *The Christian Priest Today*, p 22, quoting Psalm 106:15)

It is easy to sit back and let the leaders of the world take the blame and avoid looking at our own complicity in the state of the world. Likewise, it is easy to read Mark's account as referring just to events in the past and failing to notice that Jesus' words apply as much to ourselves. If the End is now and always,

then the time has come to face up honestly and humbly to the
signs of judgement, because only if we do will we be saved.
Mark leaves us in no doubt that reconciliation is costly work,
and those who do the work of God today must, like Jesus, pay
the price that this work requires. Writing to the Colossians, Paul
describes his own suffering as a continuation of the suffering of
Christ, 'completing what still remains for Christ to suffer in my
own person.' (Colossians 1:24) God found the shepherds of
Israel wanting, and came himself in search of his sheep. He is
still among us, offering us a new spirit and a new heart as he did
2000 years ago, and graciously he waits on our response.

VI

Son of God
Chapters 14-16

Introduction

Reading the story of the Passion my mind goes back to the year 2000 when I saw it acted out at the Passion Play in Oberammergau. Seeing the drama unfold in front of you is quite a different experience to hearing it read, bringing home that it was a real event with people who feel and think and behave like we do. The priests and Pilate more concerned to preserve their power than to heed the truth; the disciples confused and afraid when put to the test; the crowd happy to enjoy the moment, making use of any opportunity to vent their anger, but in the end unmoved and uninvolved. These were real events and the story has to be experienced, because it was the experience of living through these events that convinced the disciples that all that Jesus had said about himself was true.

Mark lets the story speak for itself. He does not embroider it, adding bits and pieces like Matthew and Luke; his account is stark. It is said that he was there and we can sense the impression it made upon him. His one description of the atmosphere says it all: 'Darkness fell over the whole land.' He records only one word from the cross, the most anguished and hopeless. The night before in the garden of Gethsemane he tells us that as Jesus went to pray 'horror and anguish overwhelmed him', and he said to Peter, James and John: 'My heart is ready to break with grief.' And going on a little further alone he utters the agonised prayer: 'Take this cup from me ...' There is no ministering angel as we find in Luke's account, and at the crucifixion there is no penitent thief; Jesus utters no words of faith from the cross, no prayer for the forgiveness of his executioners; there is no conversation with John and Mary, as in John's account; no final cry, 'It is finished!' At the moment of death the curtain of the Temple is torn in two, but there is no earthquake, no dead rising from their graves as Matthew's records.

To understand Mark we have to take away all that the other gospels add. In Mark's Passion Jesus is broken, at the end of his faith, terrifyingly alone. All his companions have fled – one in Gethsemane even risking the shame of nakedness rather than be associated with Jesus. On the cross the bystanders mock him; those crucified with him revile him, and the chief priests and the scribes laugh at his suffering: 'He saved others, but he cannot save himself.' Jesus dies completely overwhelmed by events; his head bowed not in faith, but in despair: 'My God, my God, why have you forsaken me?' This starkness is hard to take. It is not surprising that the later gospel writers softened the story. I found myself wanting to soften it. But Mark has led us to expect this conclusion. Time and again Mark points out that Jesus foretold what was to happen. After the transfiguration he said to the disciples that the scriptures foretold that the Son of Man was to endure great suffering and be treated with contempt. The story of the Passion is what Mark has been leading up to, and central to the Passion is a death, a death that is central to the whole gospel.

Good Friday is the pivotal day of the Christian year; the most important day, the most holy day, because it was on this day that sin was overcome by the sacrifice of Jesus on the cross. Good Friday is the Christian Day of Atonement. The resurrection on Easter Day gloriously confirms the divine nature of Jesus' sacrificial death; but without the death there could be no resurrection; without the sacrifice there could be no atonement; without the passion there could be no victory. St Paul would not let his Christian converts forget the centrality of the death of Jesus. Writing to the Corinthians about the Eucharist he said, 'For every time you eat this bread and drink the cup, you proclaim the death of the Lord, until he comes.' (1 Corinthians 11:26) Without the death there would be no resurrection, no forgiveness, no gift of the Holy Spirit, no church, no communion.

Some Christians go from Palm Sunday to Easter Day without going through Good Friday and the preceding days of Holy Week. Mark would be astonished at this; he would protest that you cannot short-cut the process. The truth cannot be grasped by the mind alone; it requires the understanding of the whole person: intellect, emotion, and intuition. To be grasped it has to be experienced, and even then it cannot be fully understood. Mark tells the story in detail because he wants it to be an experience for us as it was for him. As you read the final section of the gospel, remember that 'gospel' means 'good news'; what Jesus achieved on the cross, he achieved for you; through his death your forgiveness is secured.

1. Anointed
Read Mark 14:1-11
Mark begins the final section of his gospel with a dark warning: the chief priests and the scribes were looking for a way to seize Jesus and put him to death. They have failed to take him by day, so they must take him by night. Mark then inserts the beautiful story of the woman who anointed Jesus with costly perfume, 'pure oil of nard' Mark is careful to point out. (Nard was an unguent made from a rare Indian plant and was much prized in the ancient world.) This story exists in slightly different forms in all the gospels and has no fixed place in the narrative. Mark places it here, interrupting the main story of conflict and betrayal, with deliberate purpose: it illustrates what Jesus was really about. It shows the character of the man whom the leaders were determined to kill, and it adds a poignancy to his final days. Isaiah had prophesied that the Servant would not break a bruised reed, or snuff out a smouldering wick. He would open eyes that were blind, bring captives out of prison, and plant justice on earth (Isaiah 42:1-7). His vision was of justice established through compassion, and this story puts flesh and blood on that prophecy.

Mark does not say who the woman was, but she must have been someone whose life had been touched by Jesus. Feasts

were often open occasions, and so access to the house would
have been easy. As she poured the costly perfume over Jesus'
head the other guests were indignant: 'Why this waste?' they
protested, 'The perfume might have been sold for more than
three hundred denarii and the money given to the poor.' And
they began to scold her. Their reaction seems natural enough,
but they had missed the point, and Jesus will have none of it.
'Leave her alone,' he says, 'Why make trouble for her? It is a fine
thing she has done for me.' And he adds, perhaps surprisingly
to our ears, 'You have the poor among you always, and you can
help them whenever you like; but you will not always have me.'
And then he interprets her action: 'She has done what lay in her
power; she has anointed my body in anticipation of my burial.'
Jesus thus invites those around the table to look beyond the
deed to the reality to which it points – the same invitation implicit
in Jesus' miracles.

Her action was an expression of worship; she had seen the
truth about Jesus and sensing his imminent death she had offered him a costly gift. The woman had come to see Jesus as em-
bodying God's love and forgiveness in a way that those who
had kept the law meticulously had not; and she had expressed
her devotion in a very physical act of worship that united inner
intention and outward action, an offering of the whole person,
body as well as heart and mind – the very thing that Jesus found
missing in the Temple. In the house of Simon the Leper his
guests saw both true worship and true forgiveness; all that Jesus
has taught about the way to God and the character of God is
demonstrated before them. This moving encounter also shows
clearly who Jesus is. 'Messiah' means 'the anointed one', and the
anointing was on the head. By making it clear that it was Jesus'
head that was anointed (in some versions it is his feet), Mark in-
dicates clearly the meaning of the coming passion. 'He who was
the object of the guile and malice of the Jewish authorities and of
the treachery of Judas, was at the same time rightly the object of
love and devotion as Messiah.' (D. E. Nineham, *The Gospel of
Mark*, p 373) John identifies the woman as Mary of Bethany, the

sister of Lazarus and Martha, who sat at Jesus' feet listening to him as he taught. If so, the story rings true: his words had touched her heart, his power had raised her brother from the dead; she knew that Jesus was the Messiah, and now, sensing that his death was imminent, she worshipped him with all that she had. In stark contrast Judas leaves Simon's house with betrayal in his heart. He will receive money for his evil deed.

'You will not always have me,' said Jesus to the guests. It was their relationship with him that was decisive, not their concern for economy, nor indeed for the poor. The woman's overflowing generosity reflects the overflowing generosity of God, and she did what was in her power to respond to what God had done for her. The guests needed to learn the same lesson, and perhaps we do also. We often give generous, even lavish presents to those whom we love, doing what is in our power to respond to what they have done for us and what they mean to us. Reflect today on how you respond to God. Is your response to him as generous as it is to those whom you love?

2. Remembered
Read Mark 14:12-25
Every year the Jews celebrated the Passover, the festival that recalled the Exodus, the mighty act of God that delivered them from slavery in Egypt. Through that mighty act God made a covenant with Israel through which they became his people. The covenant was sealed through the shed blood of the Passover lambs. It was a new beginning, and every Jew was enjoined to keep the feast. On the night before he died Jesus kept the feast with his disciples. Earlier that day two of them were led through the narrow streets of Jerusalem by a man carrying a jar of water. He would have been quickly recognised because water-jars were usually carried by women, an unknown friend like the owner of the donkey, whose generosity has been recorded rather than his name. Jesus once said, 'Foxes have their holes and birds their roosts; but the Son of Man has nowhere to lay his head.' (Luke 9:58) As a travelling preacher with no permanent

home, he was dependent on the generosity of his friends for all that he needed.

The disciples were led to a large upper room, furnished and made ready, and in that room they prepared the Passover supper. At the end of the meal Jesus led his disciples to the Garden of Gethsemane. It's a long walk; and if you do it in the rain, as I did many years ago, you arrive soaked. There in Gethsemane he is betrayed and arrested; then he is taken back across the city to the high priest's house, not far from the upper room. When morning breaks he is taken on another long walk to the Praetorium, where he is flogged and handed over to be crucified. And then a final, utterly exhausting walk to Calvary. In the space of a few hours Jesus walked back and forth across the city four times. For Jesus these events followed one another without interruption; there was no rest or refreshment save for that last meal with the disciples in the upper room.

Each evangelist tells the story of that meal in his own way, and Mark places it between two stories of betrayal. (When Mark does this it is a way of interpreting the event. The meal points to the way in which the betrayal of God by his people will be overcome; it is the sign in time of what God has accomplished eternally.) Judas has already been to the chief priests and arranged to hand Jesus over. Aware of this, or knowing what was likely to be in Judas' heart, during the meal Jesus says that one of those eating with him will betray him. They all protest, 'Surely you do not mean me?' Their question is evasive; in their hearts they are not sure how far they will be able to keep with him, and so they try to cover their guilt. It is a common response, often learned in childhood and perpetuated in adult life. Directly challenged we give the 'right' answer, covering up our unworthy feelings. Jesus says it *is* one of them, 'who is dipping into the bowl with me'. At the end of the meal he tells them that they will desert him, 'You will all lose faith.' Peter protests, 'Everyone else may lose faith, but I will not.' Jesus tells Peter that he will deny him three times, but Peter insists, 'Even if I have to die with you, I will never disown you.' As the story unfolds, first Judas, then the rest, and finally Peter desert him. At the meal Mark does not record the command, 'Do this in remembrance of me,' but a fateful valediction: 'Truly I tell you: never again shall I drink of the fruit of the vine until that day when I drink it new in the kingdom of God.' These are the words of someone about to undergo a great travail. Through this travail his relationship with his companions will be transformed, and he forswears the fruit of the vine until that time has come. As he speaks Jesus knows that through his sacrifice God will make a New Covenant with his people, another new beginning, that his life has anticipated and which his blood will seal. True to his teaching this new beginning will extend beyond Israel to the Gentiles.

When Jesus sat down with his disciples he was aware of the imminence of his death because he made that meal a symbol of its significance. The bread was his body, soon to be broken on the cross, the wine was his blood, soon to be poured out in sacrifice. In later years Paul would insist upon this interpretation of the Eucharist: 'Every time you eat this bread and drink the cup, you proclaim the death of the Lord, until he comes.' (1 Corinthians 11.26) The Eucharist 'proclaims' the death of the Lord. The Greek word used to describe what happens in the Eucharist is *anamnesis*, which means to make effective in the present an event from the past – present now as it was then; potent in all its power. We lack a word to convey this sense adequately. 'Remembrance' is too weak; 're-present', making present again, better conveys the meaning. While we await his coming, however we understand it, when we gather around the Lord's table like the first disciples, we do not simply keep alive the memory of Jesus, nor simply recall why he died; we make real among us the power of his death, his atoning sacrifice. And because he has invited us to his table, a sign (as we saw in Chapter 3) of reconciliation, we receive for ourselves the gift that his sacrifice made possible, his greatest gift, the forgiveness of sins.

God's forgiveness is freely, even prodigally, offered, but whether it transforms our lives depends upon our response. Love cannot be forced upon another, and God has willed only to work with our co-operation; as St Augustine said, 'Without him we cannot: without us he will not.' He looks for more than a grudging acceptance that we ought to lend a hand; he looks for a generous response like that of the unknown householder who gave up the best room in his house for Jesus and his companions. As you reflect today on the connection between Jesus' death and the celebration of the Eucharist, think particularly about St Paul's interpretation. Ask yourself also whether, in Archbishop Cranmer's words, you offer yourself as 'a reasonable, holy and lively sacrifice'? Does it feel to you as though we are proclaiming the Lord's death and receiving his gift of forgiveness?

3. Betrayed
Read Mark 14:26-52
The walk from the Upper Room to the Garden of Gethsemane takes you first through the Jewish Quarter of the Old City of Jerusalem, then down a steep hillside, across the brook Kidron, and into the garden which is on the lower slopes of the Mount of Olives. It is an olive orchard, and an imposing church, the Church of All Nations, has been built there. Inside the church the focal point is a large rock, the Rock of the Agony (now surrounded by a low railing), which is hallowed as the place where Jesus threw himself on the ground and prayed, 'Abba, Father, all things are possible to you; take this cup from me. Yet not my will but yours.' In the evening away from the crowds it is a very moving place, and kneeling in prayer around the rock brings home the full anguish that Jesus felt at the onset of his passion.

As they arrive Jesus says to the disciples, 'Sit here while I pray', and then to his closest companions, Peter, James and John, he expresses the full extent of his feelings, 'My heart is ready to break with grief; stop here, and stay awake.' We need to let the full weight of Mark's words speak to us: 'Horror and anguish overwhelmed him.' The Jesus we have met in Mark's gospel is not one to be overwhelmed. He has been in control, the cause of astonishment and anger; but now things are different. The full reality of what he must endure comes upon him, even to the extent that he prays that there might be another way. We see here the cost of reconciliation. The One to whom obedience to God was meat and drink asking to be spared, but even so, willing to obey. The contrast with the disciples is telling, as they succumb to their feelings and fall asleep. No doubt they wanted to stay awake as Jesus had asked, but they just could not manage to do so: the divine strength in Jesus is contrasted with human weakness, as Jesus said, 'The spirit is willing, but the flesh is weak.' This will be within the experience of us all. The flesh often seems to have a mind of its own, as Paul knew: 'The good which I want to do, I fail to do; but what I do is the wrong which is against my will.' (Romans 7:19) We know these days from depth psychology how we are driven by deep, hidden desires and impulses, and part of human growth into mature adulthood is to become aware of these hidden forces. Naming them enables us to use them creatively; strengthening the flesh is part of our spiritual growth. It is too easy to be critical of the disciples – would we have behaved any differently? – rather we should see this episode in the garden as a picture of all that Jesus came to do, bearing our weaknesses and offering himself for us: 'Sit here while I pray.' It is by allowing Jesus to pray within us, aligning our will with God's great and loving Will, that the flesh and the spirit become one.

And so the story comes to its brutal conclusion. The threat that Jesus presented to the authorities is clear from the arrangements made for his arrest. This is not regular police work, the apprehension of a trouble-maker by a couple of officers. Judas comes accompanied by a crowd, armed with swords and cudgels. The arrest has all the marks of the overkill typical of state action against dissidents. We have seen this use of force time and again; it is routine in police states, and it happens in Britain too. This is the arrest of someone perceived as an enemy of the state. 'Seize him,' says Judas, 'and get him safely away.' Jesus challenges his captors, 'Do you take me for a robber, that you have come out with swords and cudgels to arrest me? Day after day I have been among you teaching in the temple, and you did not lay hands on me.' But Jesus is too popular for this to be done openly, and so the authorities act in a lonely place in the dead of night. Jesus spoke about those who prefer darkness to light because they know that their deeds are evil, and now that evil surrounds him. He is betrayed by a kiss, the most intimate sign of friendship. Evil seeks to mask its true nature; so in Gethsemane betrayal wears the mask of love.

There is much here to ponder, and many parallels with our own experience. As you reflect try to imagine yourself there in the garden with Jesus. Sense the atmosphere, the feelings; see the arrival of Judas and the soldiers. Place yourself in the scene. What does it feel like? How do you react?

4. Condemned
Read Mark 14:53-15:20

Having made their move the authorities lose no time. Jesus is led away to the High Priest's house. It has been well planned. Even as they arrive the members of the Council are assembling – and in the dead of night. Mark tells us that the proceedings began with an attempt 'to find some evidence against Jesus to warrant a death sentence'. Clearly this was not a proper trial. The outcome was already decided; what was needed was some pretext to justify that outcome, something that would make it defensible, something that the Council could use to explain it to the people. Again, we are familiar with these tactics. They are widely used, even in democratic regimes – there was more than a hint of them in the way the weapons inspectors were used in Iraq. Even so, the chief priests and the elders were not wicked men, leading criminal lives or brutally oppressing their people. But they were powerful men, and they were convinced both of the rightness of their position, and that they were acting for the common good. But they were also men who knew that their own position was threatened. These are ideal conditions for evil to take root. Our lower nature comes to the aid of our good intentions, and so we come to think that the end justifies the means.

The threat that Jesus posed to the priests and scribes was temporal as well as spiritual; he threatened the very foundations of their authority. He struck at the root of the established order, and he was winning over the hearts and minds of the people. Like every elite in history, the priests and the scribes considered their interests and the national interest to be the same, and that to overthrow the established order would be a disaster for the nation. Jesus had to go. But they had to have some evidence, and Jesus refused to answer the accusations put against him. Finally, the High Priest asked him a direct question: 'Are you the Messiah?' For the first time in Mark's gospel he replies equally directly, he says, 'I am.' Those two words sealed his fate. They had their evidence.

Outside in the courtyard another direct question receives an evasive answer. Another trial is taking place, a trial of loyalty, and here it is the accusers who know the truth. Peter, who had said he would never desert Jesus, is looked in the face by a maid and accused, 'You were with this man from Nazareth, this Jesus.' No doubt fearing that he too might be arrested, Peter denies it: 'I know nothing, I have no idea what you are talking about.' The accusation is repeated and so is the denial; then others join in. Peter has had the courage to follow Jesus this far, and at the end of his life he will give his life for his Lord, but right now his faith is too new and the turn of events too sudden: he is not ready for martyrdom. As the pressure increases so his denials become more vehement, he starts to curse, and with an oath he says, 'I do not know this man you are talking about.' Jesus had not won the battle for hearts and minds. If his chief disciple could so easily be made to deny him, the people also could be won over.

At the first opportunity Jesus is brought to Pilate, who alone has power to impose the death penalty. Pilate may be the representative of imperial Rome, but day to day he has to live with the priests and some sort of accommodation with them is essential to the preservation of order – and disorder was perhaps the greatest fear for the Romans. So he is already complicit, and has agreed to hear the case at an early hour. Pilate's contempt for the people he governs is clear in his question to Jesus. He asks, 'Are you the king of the Jews?' not, 'Are you king of Israel?' 'King of the Jews' is an expression of contempt, and the question is mocking, as though Pilate said, with heavy irony: 'You are the king of the Jews?' Jesus returns the irony, saying in effect, 'You said it.' And to Pilate's astonishment Jesus says nothing more.

Clearly Pilate does not believe Jesus to be guilty of anything deserving the death penalty. Mark says it is out of spite that Jesus had been brought before him, and so he tries to release him. But the priests have done their work and have turned the crowd around; they ask for Barabbas. When Pilate protests it becomes even more important for the people to have their way; it is they who choose who shall be released, not the Governor. Pilate may hold them in contempt, but he cannot ignore them if he wants to maintain order. Their object now is to get Pilate to do what they want, to humiliate the occupying power; thoughts of God and the freedom that Jesus offered are forgotten. Winning is now the name of the game. Pilate is not really interested in justice; his aim is to avoid disorder. And who can blame him? As we have seen in Iraq, civil disorder can be more terrifying than war. So to prevent a riot he hands Jesus over to be crucified.

The soldiers who now take Jesus in hand are a coarse lot. Normally subject to constricting military discipline they are now unleashed, and take out their anger and resentment on a conquered adversary. Like the servants of the High Priest a few hours before, they spit upon him, blindfold him and beat him. Jesus is abused by Gentile and Jew alike. They treat him like a plaything. Mockingly they dress and undress him at will; in their hands he is an object; powerless. Terry Waite and others taken hostage received the same treatment. This brutality seems routine in terrorism; but those who oppose it are no better, as we have seen from the shocking pictures of the abuse of Iraqi prisoners in Abu Ghraib prison. It happens too in the home. This is the evil present in child abuse and domestic violence. There was an item on the news two years ago about the trade in women for prostitution in eastern Europe. We saw one woman being touched and felt like goods for sale, an object in the power of men. It is not just the coarse who do these things, it's the civilised too. There is a dark side to every soul, and in the right conditions its evil is released.

The trials of Jesus are not about wicked men devising evil schemes, but about good men giving in to their dark side. As you reflect today, pray Jesus' words, 'Lead me not into tempt-ation but deliver me from evil.'

5. Crucified
Read Mark 15:21-39

'Then they led him out to crucify him.' The way to Golgotha led across the city from the Praetorium through a warren of narrow, winding alleys. The victim is close enough to the bystanders for them to strike him, trip him up, spit upon him. When Jesus re-quires help they pick another victim, Simon of Cyrene, someone from another country, not from the city like themselves; another stranger they could kick around. The abuse continues after Jesus has been nailed to the cross. The people jeer at him: 'He saved others but he cannot save himself. Let the Messiah, the king of Israel, come down now from the cross. If we see that, we shall believe.' Mark says the priests and the scribes joined in, jesting with one another. This is about as low as you can get: laughing as your victim suffers.

Mark brings out the cruel irony in the story. The opponents of Jesus speak the truth. The questions that are put to him can be read in Greek as statements. The chief priest says, 'You are the Christ, the Son of the Blessed'; Pilate greets him with, 'You are the king of the Jews.' The soldiers dress him up as a king; the passers-by congratulate him as the one who destroys the Temple and builds it again in three days; and finally when he is dead the centurion – in contempt rather than faith – declares him to be the Son of God. It is all true. Jesus knows it to be true. It

is the truth that mocks him. 'Jesus [is] destroyed by the contradiction between who he believes himself to be, and what is happening to him. He is God's Son, yet he is being put to death. The
contradiction is driven into him by the mocking of his opponents.' (John Fenton, *More about Mark*, p 65) God does not inter-
vene to save him. There is darkness over the land, and in the
darkness Jesus utters in anguish the one cry recorded by Mark,
'My God, my God, why have you forsaken me?' His life ends
with a question. In this cry there is a terrifying aloneness; Jesus
no longer feels that close communion with the Father that he has
had throughout his life. Bearing the weight of the sin of the
world he experiences the alienation of the world from God. The
Son of God feels forsaken by God. The cup is not taken away.

Jesus, we say, was obedient unto death, even death on a cross
(Philippians 2:8). The words fall easily from our lips. Mark
shows us what they really mean. And it is a severe test of faith.
Can we believe in a God who does not save by miracles, and
who provides no proof that the good news is true? A God who
does not come and fix it, and make it alright? If we see God
standing by while his Son suffers excruciating pain and mental
torment, requiring this as some sort of price or satisfaction for
his outrage at the sinfulness of the world, then I do not think we
can believe in him. Such a God is a monster. But if we see God
himself in Jesus bearing the pain and the grief of the sin of the
world, then we can believe in him, because we know from our
own experience that this is what reconciliation requires.

When we are divided against one another, whether individ-
uals, groups, or nations, reconciliation requires a peace-maker.
We appoint people specially to undertake this work, e.g. diplo-
mats, industrial conciliators, and marriage counsellors. This
work is lonely, isolating, painful and costly. The peace-maker
has to give of him- or herself in building the bridge of reconciliation. Peace making involves self-sacrifice, putting yourself on
the line, accepting that you will be hurt as you bear the anger,
the hurt, the lack of trust. If this is true of the sons of men, how
much more is it true of the Son of Man? Jesus was the suffering

servant who built the bridge of reconciliation between God and his creation that no one else could build. Jesus' death meant life for Barabbas, and 'Barabbas' means 'Everyman'. 'Through him,' wrote St Paul, 'God chose to reconcile the whole universe to himself, making peace though the shedding of his blood on the cross.' (Colossians 1:20)

As Jesus died Mark says he gave a loud cry, 'and the curtain of the Temple was torn in two from top to bottom.' The curtain separated the sanctuary from the rest of the Temple, protecting it from view and, symbolically, protecting God from view. Only the priests were permitted to go beyond it. Jesus' death rends the curtain and removes the barrier. From now on all can see God at work, as those who behold the cross see him at work, and through this death on the cross all may now approach him. There was darkness over the land, and in that darkness God was at work.

As you reflect today, think about the sins of those who condemned Jesus: cruel thoughts and actions; treating people as objects, taking pleasure in their misfortune; showing prejudice against those who are different; cutting corners – especially the moral ones – in order to achieve our aims; not being true to our friends or our principles, especially when our security is threatened. As you have experienced this story perhaps you have seen a bit of yourself in those who condemned Jesus. Perhaps you remained on the sidelines, uninvolved. Either way, you might like to pray the prayer of the penitent thief, 'Jesus, remember me when you come into your kingdom.'

6. Buried
Read Mark 15:40-47

It is evening; it is all over. The crowds have gone. They have put away their mocking words, their vengeful actions. Life has to go on; respectability reclaims them. But a number of women and some of the disciples who had come up to Jerusalem with Jesus remain, among them Mary of Magdala and perhaps Jesus' mother. (Mark mentions 'Mary the mother of James and Joses', who were Jesus' brothers: 6:3.) Mark says the women 'had all followed him and looked after him when he was in Galilee.' Here at the end we have a poignant insight into the love in which Jesus was held and how he was supported as he travelled. These are the women who will come to the tomb the next day to offer one final act of love, anointing him in death as he was anointed in life at the house of Simon the leper. Meanwhile, as evening falls, another follower is moved to offer his own act of love. Joseph of Arimathea 'bravely went to Pilate and asked for the body of Jesus.' And he was given leave to take it away. Joseph was a member of the Council that had condemned Jesus for blasphemy. How did he feel about that decision? Perhaps he argued against it; perhaps he felt that opposition was useless; but his own part in it haunts him; he must make some amends.

What we do for someone when they die speaks not only of love but of our moral nature. As I write we have seen pictures of bodies left floating in the flood waters of New Orleans, and those left abandoned by the roadside in Iraq. It is shocking. A human body is not to be thrown away as just so much garbage. Jesus cannot be left hanging on the cross; the least Joseph can do is to ensure that his body is not humiliated any more, and so he takes it away for burial. And then there are all the mixed feelings that death brings to the surface. Someone dies; there have been problems between us, but now we have lost the opportunity to put things right. At least we can honour them in their death, and express our true feelings. Joseph was a man who looked forward to the kingdom of God. Like Jesus, he was living in hope for the time when God will be king, but he was unable, because of his position, to show how he hoped. And now Jesus has been taken away. In a final act of loving service, tenderly he wraps the body in a linen sheet and lays it in a tomb cut out of the rock.

The gospels are silent as to what happened between the burial and the resurrection. The belief developed that Jesus descended into hell to rescue the dead, the so-called 'harrowing of hell', and this belief is part of the Apostles' Creed. It has inspired some wonderful art, but of its truth we cannot tell. But something happened. On this day of waiting, in his apparent absence, God performs his greatest, his most mysterious work: a new way is opened by which those who have turned away from God may return to him and be healed. How this is done we cannot know, for this work is accomplished in the abyssal depths of God, the utterly unknowable aspect of the Father. All we know is that it was accomplished and that through it we receive God's grace.

Think about Joseph. He stands for all believers; he stands for us. He receives the dead, ruined remains of Jesus, God's present to the world, its ransom, the price of our reconciliation with God (John Fenton, *More about Mark*, p 69). As the scapegoat carried away the sins of the Israelites into the wilderness where they were lost for ever, so Jesus takes our sins to the grave and buries them with him. As Isaiah said, 'By his humiliation my servant will justify many; ... it is their guilt he bears.' (Isaiah 53:11)

7. Resurrected

Read Mark 16:1-8

Mark ends his gospel on a dramatic note. It seems unfinished, and there was a time when it was believed that the original ending had been lost, but today the general view is that Mark did end his story with the women overwhelmed by what they had seen and heard. The last twelve verses are clearly the work of other hands: they do not follow naturally from verse 8. Mark says clearly that the women went away from the tomb and 'said nothing to anyone, for they were afraid'. They disobeyed the instruction of the young man to pass on his message to Peter and the disciples. It is difficult to continue beyond this 'with a further story that flows on from what has been said without hiatus, repetition or contradiction.' (John Fenton, *More about Mark*, p 15) Mark's gospel only feels unfinished because the other gospels do add further stories, and we know what happened next! But Mark's abrupt ending is consistent with the whole tenor of his gospel. Time and again we have seen people set at naught by the divine power and teaching of Jesus, and now, at the end, the women are completely overwhelmed by their experience.

They had gone early to the tomb to anoint Jesus, a final act of love for the one who had loved them and taught them, and who had brought God alive for them unlike any other teacher. It had not been possible to anoint him when he died, or on the next day because it was the Sabbath, and so they came at the earliest opportunity to make good the omission, wondering who would roll away the stone. Their feelings of apprehension must have quickened when they saw that the stone had been moved, and it must have taken some courage to enter the tomb, fearing what they might find: had the body been stolen, or desecrated? But instead of a body they see sitting there 'a young man wearing a white robe' (presumably an angel), who speaks to them. Angels were believed to represent the presence of God: no wonder they are dumbfounded by the experience, and they 'ran away from the tomb, trembling with amazement.' Clearly they were not expecting the resurrection. Jesus had spoken about it, but they had not really taken in what he was saying, after all the idea of resurrection, let alone the reality, is beyond the limits of our experience. No wonder they ran away, afraid to speak. Mark's gospel ends as it began. His account of the resurrection is spare and awesome; there is the same lack of understanding that affected the disciples; the same sense of mystery around the figure of Jesus. The effect that Jesus had on people in his life prefigures the effect he will have on them in his new life.

'He has been raised; he is not here. Look, there is the place where they laid him. But go and say to his disciples and to Peter: "He is going on ahead of you into Galilee: there you will see him, as he told you".' The words of the young man express the resurrection faith of the church. 'He has been raised': the resurrection is an act of God, not something Jesus did for himself. He is not restored to this life, like Lazarus, but to a new order of existence entirely, beyond the limitations of time and space. It is both continuous with this life, and utterly different from it. This is the sign that 'God was in Christ reconciling the world to himself, no longer holding people's misdeeds against them.' (2 Corinthians 5:19) 'The resurrection,' says Richard Harries, 'is God's unqualified seal of approval of all that Jesus was and stood for. The authority with which he taught, his claim to forgive sins, the identification of his outreach to sinners with God's love for us, his relationship of a son to the Father – all this is revealed to be grounded in God himself.' (Richard Harries, *Being a Christian*, p 23) The resurrection does not make these things true; they were always true. The resurrection is the clearest demonstration of their truth. The resurrection is the most profound statement of what God is like. The eternal movement is from life, through death, to new life. We know this in our everyday experience of growth and maturity. Life is a series of little deaths which lead us into a fuller, more complete life. Growing up means losing the securities of childhood, the certainties of adolescence, the ambitions of adulthood. Accepting this with grace is part of growing into what God made us to become. It is one of the deepest Christian insights that this personal movement is one with God's eternal movement. If we learn to trust it, it is our intimate proof that God's purposes of love can never fail. In the resurrection God says to us, 'You can trust me with your life.'

Ending as it does, Mark's gospel is an invitation to trust. He offers no proof that Jesus was raised, instead he invites us to believe that just as all that Jesus said about himself, especially his death, was fulfilled, so his promise of new life will also be fulfilled. He teaches us not to depend on reassurance in the present, but to trust in God to whom all things are possible: it is his power, not our efforts, that will transform our lives. The women, like the male disciples, the religious leaders and the Romans, all failed. But God makes use of human failure; as St Paul said, we have treasure in earthen vessels, but that does not matter for God's power is made perfect in weakness. This is Mark's Good News. 'Mark's gospel invites the reader into a new world, where we are no longer the victims of our upbringing and the accidents of our personalities, because there is a God who is omnipotent; and he reveals his omnipotence in the story Mark tells of human ignorance, misunderstanding, fear and weakness.' (John Fenton, *More about Mark*, p 5) Like the women, we are to keep vigil, to wait and pray for the dawn, and meanwhile to offer our service to God, that his kingdom may come on earth as in heaven

Mark's gospel is like an unfinished symphony; it is up to others to write the remaining movements. The story continued through Peter and Paul and the other apostles; through Benedict and Francis and the saints down the ages; through countless un-named followers who have believed in Jesus not just as the Son of Man, but as the Son of God, and who have trusted him with their lives, and seen their lives transformed. In Jesus God offers us a new beginning, just as he offered the people of Israel. In him God opened a door to heaven. 'The time has come,' Jesus said, 'repent and believe the gospel.' God never ceases from his work of reconciliation, but there are times when the open door seems to face us more squarely. His call to us never ceases, but there are times when we hear it more clearly, calling us to be part of the next movement in his unfinished symphony. Wherever we are on the Way there is always another step to take, and the moment will come when we must take it. Perhaps this Lenten journey has been such a moment, and the time has come.

Books referred to

Louise Creighton (ed), *The Life and Letters of Mandell Creighton* (Longman: London, 1904) [The letter dated 3rd April 1887.]

The Rule of St Benedict, translated by David Parry, OSB (Darton, Longman & Todd: London, 1984)

Mother Mary Clare, SLG, *Encountering the Depths* (SLG Press: Fairacres, Oxford, 1973)

Jane Collier, 'Contemporary culture and the role of economics' in Hugh Montefiore (ed), *The Gospel and Contemporary Culture* (Mowbray: London, 1992)

John Fenton, *More about Mark* (SPCK: London, 2001)

Bede Frost, *Lent with St Benedict* (Kevin Mayhew Ltd: Rattlesden, Bury St Edmunds, 1997)

Richard Harries, *Being a Christian* (A. R. Mowbray & Co Ltd: Oxford, 1981)

Basil Hume, OSB, *Light in the Lord – Reflections on Priesthood* (St Paul Publications: Slough, 1991)

John Macquarrie, *The Faith of the People of God – A Lay Theology* (SCM Press Ltd: London, 1972)

C. F. D. Moule, *The Gospel According to Mark – The Cambridge Bible Commentary on the New English Bible* (Cambridge University Press: Cambridge, 1965)

Owen Nankivell, *Economics, Society and Values* (Avebury / Ashgate Publishing Ltd: Aldershot, 1995)

D. E. Nineham, *Saint Mark* – Pelican New Testament Commentaries (Penguin Books Ltd: Harmondsworth, 1963)

Moshe Pearlman, *In the Footsteps of Moses*, (Oliphants: London, 1976)

Michael Ramsay, *The Christian Priest Today* (SPCK: London, 1972)

John A. T. Robinson, *Can We Trust the New Testament?* (A. R. Mowbray & Co Ltd: Oxford, 1977)

M. Jack Suggs, Katharine Doob Salkenfeld, James R Mueller (eds), *The Oxford Study Bible, REB version* (Oxford University Press: New York, 1992)

Victor de Waal, *What is the Church?* (SCM Press Ltd: London, 1969)